W9-BZV-821

Principals and Counselors Partnering for Student Success

Edited by
Faith Connolly and Nancy Protheroe

Because research and information make the difference.

Educational Research Service
1001 North Fairfax Street, Suite 500 • Alexandria, VA 22314-1587
Phone: 703-243-2100 • Toll Free: 800-791-9308
Fax: 703-243-1985 • Toll Free: 800-791-9309
Email: ers@ers.org • Web site: www.ers.org

Naviance, Inc.
1850 K Street NW, Suite 1000 • Washington, DC 20006
Phone: 202-349-2700 • Toll Free: 866-337-0080
Fax: 202-349-2719 • Web site: www.naviance.com

Educational Research Service
1001 North Fairfax Street, Suite 500 • Alexandria, VA 22314-1587
Phone: 703-243-2100 • Toll Free: 800-791-9308
Fax: 703-243-1985 • Toll Free: 800-791-9309
Email: ers@ers.org • Web site: www.ers.org

Educational Research Service Educational Research Service is *the* nonprofit organization providing school leaders with essential research for effective decisions. Founded by the national school management associations, ERS is the school leader's best source for resources and data to build more successful schools. Since 1973, education leaders have utilized the ERS advantage to make the most effective school decisions in both day-to-day operations and long-range planning. Refer to the last page of this publication to learn how you can benefit from the services and resources available through an annual ERS subscription. Or visit us online at www.ers.org for a more complete picture of the wealth of preK-12 research information and tools available through ERS subscriptions and resources.

ERS Founding Organizations:
American Association of School Administrators
American Association of School Personnel Administrators
Association of School Business Officials International
National Association of Elementary School Principals
National Association of Secondary School Principals
National School Public Relations Association

Naviance, Inc.
1850 K Street NW, Suite 1000 • Washington, DC 20006
Phone: 202-349-2700 • Toll Free: 866-337-0080
Fax: 202-349-2719 • Web site: www.naviance.com

Naviance, Inc. Naviance is the leading provider of student success solutions for K-12 schools. Naviance engages students, teachers, counselors, administrators, and families in creating active, personalized success plans that promote graduation and readiness for college and the twenty-first century workplace. Naviance is the K-12 division of Hobsons, a subsidiary of DMG Information, which in turn is part of the Daily Mail and General Trust.

Library of Congress Cataloging-in-Publication Data

Principals and counselors partnering for student success/edited by Faith Connolly and Nancy Protheroe.
 p. cm.
 ISBN 978-1-931762-87-8
1. School principal-counselor relationships—United States. 2. Academic achievement—United States. I. Connolly, Faith. II. Protheroe, Nancy.
 LB1027.5.P75 2009
 371.4—dc22
                    2009032161

Editors: Faith Connolly and Nancy Protheroe
Layout & Design: Susie McKinley
Cover Design: Libby McNulty

Ordering Information: Additional copies of *Principals and Counselors Partnering for Student Success* may be purchased at the base price of $30.00 from ERS; ERS subscribers receive special subscriber discounts. Quantity discounts available. Add $4.50 or 10% of total purchase price for shipping and handling. Phone orders accepted with Visa, MasterCard, or American Express. Stock No. 0770. ISBN: 978-1-931762-87-8.

Note: ERS and Naviance, Inc. are responsible for this publication; no approval or endorsement by ERS founders is implied.

Contents

Introduction

Faith Connolly and Nancy Protheroe

Development of *Principals and Counselors Partnering for Student Success* began with recognition of the positive impact a strong principal-counselor partnership can have on schools and students. While most principals and counselors would, if asked, agree that such a relationship is important, many haven't had either the time or opportunity to have conversations with their counterparts about what a really effective relationship would look like in practice—or of the ways in which it could support schools and students. *Principals and Counselors Partnering for Student Success* was written to provide a framework for those conversations.

Interestingly, work on the project began with a conversation. Professionals with long-term experience working in schools or in support of schools gathered to talk about school counseling. The theme was: What information—what topics—are important to principals and counselors as they meet to discuss their roles, in what ways they can support each other, and the school counseling program? There was agreement that both a conceptual framework—grounded in research and best practice—and practical examples were important. Principals and counselors would then be able to immediately move from the abstract to the conditions in their own schools. Specific

Faith Connolly, Ph.D., is Vice President of Policy and Research at Naviance, Inc. Prior to working at Naviance, she directed research and evaluation for Montgomery County Public Schools, MD, and was the Executive Assistant to the Accountability Officer of Baltimore City Public Schools. Email faith.connolly@naviance.com. Nancy Protheroe is Director of Special Research Studies at Educational Research Service. Email nprotheroe@ers.org.

topics discussed also reflected this theory-practice approach. Thus, in *Principals and Counselors Partnering for Student Success*, you'll find information on principal-counselor collaboration, creation and management of a strong counseling program, and a description of what a comprehensive developmental guidance program looks like.

Today's schools, with their increasingly diverse student populations and ever-higher achievement standards, need to use all their resources in ways that create maximum positive impact for students and student learning. A school's counseling program is one of these resources. In recognition of the importance of that resource, *Principals and Counselors Partnering for Student Success* provides a roadmap for ways principals and counselors can—through collaboration—enhance the skills and knowledge each of them brings to the partnership.

Looking Ahead

Carolyn Stone and Carol Dahir write that "exploring the potential for the school counselor/principal partnership will take this entire book and will in no way exhaust the possibilities." From one perspective, this is true. Each school—and each principal-counselor partnership—is unique and so each partnership must recognize its own challenges and also build from its own strengths. However, the chapters in this book together provide a strong framework, written from a variety of perspectives, for both conceptual and practical issues that should be addressed.

In the first chapter, "Addressing the Challenges of 21st-Century Schools Through Principal-Counselor Collaboration," Mel Riddile outlines some of the challenges schools currently face and ways that effective principal-counselor collaboration can help to address them. During his tenure as principal of a multicultural, high-needs high school, he leveraged counselor expertise to change school practices (e.g., the development of the master schedule to better serve the needs of each student in the school). The changes he made resulted in a more supportive environment for both students and staff, with his success recognized through his selection as a MetLife-NASSP Principal of the Year. In his chapter, Mel emphasizes the importance of the principal-counselor relationship, the development and use of effective functional and cross-functional teams to address student needs, and the creation of a student-centered environment.

In "Principal-Counselor Alliance for Accountability and Data Use," coauthors Carolyn Stone and Carol Dahir talk about the alliance within a framework of data-informed leadership for school improvement. The topic has been a long-term interest for both of them and has resulted in books such as *School Counselor Accountability: A Measure of Student Success* and *The Transformed School Counselor*, as well as numerous journal articles.

In their chapter, Carolyn and Carol focus on five areas where the principal-counselor partnership can use data and shared accountability to influence:

1. **Equity and the achievement gap.** By disaggregating data, counselors can work with principals to identify students left out of the success equation.

2. **System barriers.** Together they can use data to identify system-wide barriers to student success, such as underenrollment of particular groups of students in advanced level courses. Counselors can play a key role in identifying such systemic barriers and in working with district and school staff to remove them.

3. **Student aspirations and course enrollment patterns.** Good advising means providing students with information about how course selection can impact later economic opportunity.

4. **Resource brokering.** Counselors can play a leadership role in providing scholarship and financial aid advising to students and families that is both informational and that helps them to see postsecondary education as a realistic option.

5. **The instructional program.** Counselors can complement a principal's role as instructional leader by providing staff development to teachers on motivation, support, interventions, learning strategies, and encouragement. Through such involvement, counselors have a direct impact on academic achievement.

Authors Carey Dimmet, Matt Militello, and Chris Janson take an especially important perspective in "School Counselors and Principals Partnering for Achievement: What Does the Research Evidence Say?" As researchers who also have experience in schools, all three authors are ideally suited for the task of using the knowledge base to address issues of practical importance to schools.

> **Principal-Counselor Partnerships: What Works**
>
> 1. Collaboration
> 2. Shared language
> 3. Understanding of roles
> 4. Ongoing conversation
> 5. Focus on specific outcomes
> 6. Distributed leadership

Carey, Matt, and Chris identify three major strands of research—school principals and student achievement, school counselors and student achievement, and principal-counselor collaboration—with practical significance. They succinctly summarize the major lessons of each of these strands under the heading "what works." In their view, the "what works" of effective principal-counselor partnerships highlights the importance of six key elements: collaboration, the development of a shared language, an understanding of each other's roles, opportunities for ongoing conversation, agreement/focus on specific outcomes, and the existence of distributed leadership in the school.

In Chapter 4, "Beyond Serendipity: Intentional Principal and School Counselor Collaboration and Inquiry," authors Chris Janson and Matt Militello use the script of a play to model the principal-counselor partnership in a way that provides examples of how it can work, even when some staff are resistant. Through it, they demonstrate the power the relationship can have on barriers that school practices—whether formal or informal—have on social justice issues such as student access to educational programs. The example provided can help any principal think through how such a team model—

using distributed leadership and taking advantage of the expertise of all the participants—can be used to identify and address problems.

Chris and Matt then urge principals and counselors to move "beyond serendipity" and become intentional about taking the next steps that can help build this more collaborative culture:

- Formalize meetings between counselors and principals and have them focus on issues of teaching and learning.

- Develop inclusive decision-making processes.

- Engage in "scholarly collaboration" around key issues.

- Explore areas of role overlap in an effort to identify how the principal and counselor might build an ever-stronger team for school improvement.

Practical Processes for Creating an Outstanding Counseling Program in Your School

- Suggestions for hiring counselors (page 122)
- Interview questions (page 123)
- Factors to consider when hiring a director (page 124)
- Effective supervising (page 125)
- Empowering counselors to become school leaders (page 128)
- Fostering effective counselor-teacher relationships (page 131)

In Chapter 5, "A Principal's Guide to Practical Considerations in the Organization and Management of the School Counseling Program," authors Ian Martin, Hilda Lopez, and John C. Carey discuss elements critical to building and maintaining a strong counseling program. In their chapter, they mesh information about the conceptual base of a strong counseling program with practical suggestions for principals. In their words, the chapter "focuses on the little details that can have a big impact on school counseling programs and, ultimately, the larger school environment."

An interesting section in the chapter addresses the topic of supervision of the work of school counselors. The authors describe the supervision needed as being of two types—administrative supervision and clinical supervision. Suggestions are provided concerning ways to strengthen a principal's role regarding administrative supervision. However, the authors make clear counselors' need for someone other than the principal to provide clinical supervision, since "it requires specialized professional knowledge and skills in the discipline of school counseling."

What Works in the Field to Impact Student Achievement

√ Aligning work with the school improvement process
√ Using data to inform program development
√ Use of action plans such as MEASURE

In Chapter 6, "What Works in the Field: Comprehensive School Counseling Programs," authors Chris Janson and Carolyn Stone use examples from school counseling offices that applied to the American School Counselor Association (ASCA) Recognized ASCA Model Program (RAMP). These real-life examples demonstrate what effective counseling programs look like and do to impact their schools and, ultimately, student learning. The highlighted programs resulted, for example, in increased participation in AP courses, increased attention to middle school students' graduation trajectories and supports for students projected to have gaps in graduation credits, improved violence prevention and character enrichment programs for students, and collaboration with teachers to better link instruction to students' future career interests.

Finally, Chris Janson and Matt Militello wrap up the challenging agenda proposed by all the chapters' authors in "Where Do We Go From Here?" A critical piece of their chapter is the identification and discussion of "Eight Elements of Effective School Principal-Counselor Relationships." In their view, elements such as mutual value and a shared belief in interdependency "resonate throughout this book." They also provide a roadmap for principals and counselors as they work to ensure that their relationship provides effective support for a school's programs and, especially, for its students.

Take Aways, Next Steps, Your Action Plan

Mel Riddile, who wrote the first chapter of this book, described the changing counselor's role below:

> Just as the principal's role has changed from manager to instructional leader, so too has the school counselor's role changed, with these people prominent members of the school leadership team. Counselors play a critical role in the success of each student and the overall success of the school.

This former principal's view of how counselors can help schools focus on student success demonstrates that the presence of effective counselors in a school makes a principal's job easier. In addition, principals and counselors can together have a more substantial impact on student learning than either of them could separately. But, as chapter authors Chris Janson and Matt Militello make clear, a strong principal-counselor relationship is most likely to come about through intentional efforts. Principals should take the lead in identifying ways to make this happen. A variety of themes recur through the chapters in this book—collaboration, staff engagement in data use, distributed leadership, and the importance of communication. A good first step in identifying ways to make even strong principal-counselor relationships better is to use this book and these themes to guide principal-counselor conversations about what matters—both in terms of their relationships and of ways in which they can work together to ensure that every student has a successful school experience.

Chapter 1

Addressing the Challenges of 21st-Century Schools Through Principal-Counselor Collaboration

Mel Riddile

School leaders are under increasing pressure to ensure that each and every student in their charge receives a high-quality education and graduates not only on time, but ready to transition to college and the workplace. This is different than the way schools operated in the 20th century, when a school was successful as long as the majority of its students succeeded. Today's 21st-century schools are asked to ensure that *all* students succeed.

This change in focus from *some* students succeeding to *all* students succeeding comes at the same time schools are facing tightening budgets, declining revenues, and scarce resources, and at a time when students' needs are becoming more complex. English Language Learners (ELLs) are the fastest-growing segment of the school-aged

---

Mel Riddile is currently Associate Director for High School Services at the National Association of Secondary School Principals. He previously served as Principal at T.C. Williams High School in Alexandria, VA, and at J.E.B. Stuart High School in Falls Church, VA. In 2006, he was selected as the MetLife-NASSP High School Principal of the Year.

population and increasing numbers of students are identified as having disabilities. In many schools, special needs populations make up a majority of the student population. Students and their families are more mobile, which results in interrupted learning.

The readiness of students is, thus, a major concern. A recent ACT (2008) study revealed that, despite all the rhetoric relating to higher expectations for student achievement, less than 20% of all eighth-graders are on target to graduate from high school college- or workplace-ready.

> This means that more than 8 of 10 eighth-grade students do not have the knowledge and skills they need to enter high school and succeed there. ...[S]tudents who are not prepared for high school are less likely than other students to be prepared for college and career when they graduate from high school. So although the gates of high school are technically open to all students, for more than 80 percent of them the door to their futures may already be closed. (ACT, 2008)

Twentieth-century schools focused on what teachers taught. Covering material was more important than mastery, and learning time was held constant. Seat time was a measure of success. Schools were, by definition, reactive, and school was essentially a weeding-out process. Students were given an opportunity. If they didn't succeed, they had other paths that they could follow. They could go to work in factories or mills in jobs that needed little more than functional literacy.

In those 20th-century schools, demography was destiny. Even in the nation's best school systems, poverty, ethnicity, and race accurately predicted success or failure.

In today's 21st-century schools, the focus is on student learning and outcomes. What teachers teach takes a backseat to what students learn. Students are expected to improve continuously. The bell curve—some succeed, some don't, so what—has given way to the J curve—continuous, incremental improvement. Seat time has given way to personal accountability. Showing up at school every day no longer guarantees success. Finally, in the era of accountability, schools today are forced to act more proactively to ensure that each student succeeds.

Today's schools are judged by what their students know and are able to do. Local, state, and national accountability mandates send the clear message that it is no longer acceptable for significant segments of the student population to be underserved. Therefore, school leaders must redesign their schools, fundamentally alter their practice, and find different ways to proactively engage students, families, and faculties. It is no longer business as usual. Instead, schools are being tasked with finding ways to build individual plans that work for each student—mass customization.

For schools to succeed under 21st-century demands, it will be up to the people that comprise the school to adopt new styles of work. Teachers who use the same methods to teach the same lessons to students that they used 20 years ago will get the same results—some students will succeed, but many will not and, today, that is unacceptable.

School leaders who use 20th-century skills and strategies to lead today's schools will get 20th-century results, i.e., bureaucratic-style schools that successfully sorted students but left many behind. Centralized, top-down school administration is not capable of designing a personalized and customized learning plan for each student. It is a system designed to have students fall through the cracks. Just as teachers are expected to differentiate their approach to meet the unique learning needs of each student, so too will school leaders need to differentiate their approach. Leading change efforts that will recreate schools to meet the rising expectations for student success will demand a variety of leadership styles and behaviors.

Personalization also demands collaboration. One person, working alone, does not have the information or expertise to design or customize a learning plan for every student. For example, designing a schedule for an ELL may require collaboration among the administrator, counselor, English as a Second Language (ESL) teacher, and ESL department chair. In the past, schools were siloed—departments acted independently and were run by senior teachers, department chairs, and team leaders, each with their own agendas, sometimes competing with other departments for scarce resources. Schools today are defined by the efforts of high-performing teams of professionals working together to meet the needs of every student.

Great teams are the foundation of great schools. Schools of the 21st century must be less hierarchical and less top-down. Their success is dependent on the collective effort of all staff organized into functional teams focused on the success of each student. A flatter school design places a premium on collaborative leadership skills that has the intent of distributing leadership throughout the school.

Collaboration in building high-performing teams and creating a learning community that supports student success is an important by-product of principal and counselor interactions. It is the school counselor who puts the school plan into action. The moment of truth in putting lofty academic goals and aspirations for student success into practice occurs when the school counselor sits down with a student to develop an individual learning plan. Unless there is a close working relationship between the principal and counselor—a partnership, with effective communication and buy-in from all sides—the school's hopes and dreams for each student will never be realized.

In today's schools, the principal is no longer just a manager. He or she is the instructional leader of the school. The role of the school counselor has changed as well, and counselors are critical members of the school leadership team. More than ever before, counselors are actively engaged with students, parents, and faculty. Students need multiple paths to success; this need for a customized approach for each student, as well as the need to monitor testing data, a much more complicated curriculum, and a myriad of state graduation requirements, have combined to increase the complexity of the school counselor's task. This complexity increases the specialized knowledge needed by counselors and also increases the likelihood of confusion and misalignment between what the counselor does and the focus of the school.

But such confusion or misalignment doesn't have to happen. Just as teachers and departments within a school can no longer act as silos, neither can school counseling programs. Counselors must now be directly involved across all departments, disciplines, and school initiatives. They must understand the what, how, and why of literacy initiatives, technology integration efforts, and ELL and special education programs and priorities. Counselors must also understand new course sequences for at-risk students, mentoring and advisory programs, after-school tutoring opportunities, and the myriad of family and social services available to their students. The list goes on and on.

This ever-increasing complexity makes alignment of mission and function difficult for everyone, including principals and counselors. Counselors and principals must work collaboratively in a partnership to ensure consistency between the plan designed for each student and the overall mission of the school.

Personalizing the school environment creates a sense of belonging and provides students with opportunities to assume ownership over their learning. Counselors play a critical role in ensuring that the school is an inviting place that engages families as partners and aids in eliminating student anonymity. Monitoring student progress and sharing in the development of tiered intervention strategies in a timely manner allows teachers to adjust their approach and students to alter their practice collectively. It also results in less teacher frustration and greater student success.

Curriculum, instruction, and assessment are about the relationship between students and learning. Today, school leaders must redesign their schools to align instruction, school initiatives, and scarce resources in order to prepare students for success. School leaders must create schools that make it easy for students, teachers, and counselors to succeed.

One aspect of the needed redesign is a focus on the working relationship between principals and counselors. Principals and counselors must engage in a continuing dialogue that ensures a continuous loop of free-flowing information. Counselors hear from both students and teachers on the successes and failures of the curriculum. Counselors work in a data-rich environment, and using counselor-generated data for planning purposes—instead of solely for reporting—makes a difference in how schools reduce student failure. They are in a unique position to help inform instruction and assist in targeting review and remediation efforts.

A close working relationship between the principal and the counselor ensures that there is alignment between the stated desires for student academic success and actual practice. Working as a team, counselors and principals can ensure that the school is responsive to student, parent, and teacher needs and that the school has the capacity to link students' current academic preparation to their future goals.

Changing School Operations to Meet the Challenges—Some Practical Examples

Every principal already knows about the challenges schools face and has been exposed to a multitude of articles, presentations, etc., that discuss the importance of increasing staff collaboration to better address these challenges. But what are some specific ways that such collaboration—energized by a closer working relationship between the principal and counselors—might look like in a 21st-century school? In the remainder of this chapter, I offer brief descriptions of approaches a high school serving a highly diverse student body—a high school of which I was principal—used to effectively address student needs.

Moving Toward a Team Approach

When touring a 20th-century school, you might ask the staff members, "What department are you in?" In today's schools, we ask, "What teams are you on?"

In the past, schools were organized hierarchically. Decisions and information flowed in a bureaucratic, top-down manner. Hierarchies and the resultant bureaucracies are effective at making rules and procedures and standardizing practices. They are designed to control, not to get things done. These 20th-century schools were also set up to sort students for success.

The paradigm has shifted dramatically. Twenty-first-century schools must be organized to help every student graduate and to ensure every graduate is college- and workplace-ready. To do this, schools must develop a plan for each student, an approach that demands more collaboration and more specialized input from more professionals. To do this effectively, schools will need to become less hierarchical and flatter—shifting to using functional and cross-functional teams as the cornerstone of school operations. In functional teams, members share a common base of expertise. Functional teams include subject-area teams like algebra or biology as well as departmental and intradepartmental teams. The guidance and counseling team, math department, and English department are all functional teams.

A cross-functional team contains members from various functional areas and with a range of specialized expertise who come together for a common purpose. Examples of cross-functional teams include: literacy councils, school improvement teams, leadership councils, attendance committees, and grade-level teams. The members of these teams are all focused on a specific objective—working together to improve coordination and innovation across departments.

Effective teams will produce innovation and improved outcomes (e.g., higher levels of student achievement). However, establishing teams is only the first step. These teams need effective leaders. In this flatter environment, developing leaders becomes a major priority of the school principal. A flatter school design places a premium on collaborative leadership skills. Thus, school leaders must intentionally cultivate new leaders and distribute leadership throughout the school.

In the short run, the success of these teams depends on the collective effort of all staff organized into cross-functional teams who are focused on the success of each student. These teams must have the authority to act in a semi-autonomous manner and share responsibility for promoting student outcomes.

In the long run, distributed leadership is the key to sustaining changes in the school culture and organization. The fewer people who share the vision, the shorter its life. In contrast, shared leadership and a shared vision spread throughout the school will result in long-term, lasting change.

Just as the principal's role has changed from manager to instructional leader, so too has the school counselor's role changed. Counselors are now prominent members of the school leadership team and play a critical role in the success of each student and the overall success of the school. They are members of a functional team—counseling—and they lead cross-functional teams that serve to focus school and community resources on meeting student needs in both academic and nonacademic areas. Such a team is typically composed of classroom teachers, teacher-advisors, and learning specialists in developing personal learning plans.

Counselors also lead a student services team—comprised of administrators, counselors, social workers, attendance officers, a psychologist, and teacher-advisors—that focuses on the nonacademic needs of students. The primary role of the student services team is to address academic, medical, behavioral, and emotional problems, as well as other concerns, such as attendance, that interfere with a student's academic success.

The specialized knowledge and expertise needed to help every student succeed shifts the role of the counselor away from a direct service provider to that of a facilitator and coordinator of interventions. Counselors work with other team members to jointly identify conditions that interfere with learning by coordinating services to help the student become successful. One of the team members assumes "next step" responsibilities and reports to the team at the next meeting.

Student Services Team meetings in my school worked as follows:

1. As team leader, the counselor presents a student for consideration by the team.

2. Information is presented on student academic performance, discipline and attendance, behavior, health, family history, etc.

3. The student services team discusses the presenting problem and outlines possible approaches.

4.   One member of the team leaves the meeting with responsibility for the "next step."

5.   The counselor works with the team member to ensure continuity of service.

6.   The counselor continues to introduce the student at subsequent meetings until the problem is successfully resolved.

Significant improvement in the quality of our schools demands that school leaders maximize the use of the collective knowledge and expertise of the entire school staff. One person—one counselor—cannot possibly meet the specialized needs of every student without input and support from other staff members. In this team-oriented environment, counselors must take on an important leadership role.

Developing the Master Schedule Collaboratively

If you want to know what makes a teacher tick, have a conversation with that teacher about grading and examine the teacher's grading practices. Often, the way teachers grade students reveals more about them—their beliefs and attitudes, as well as what motivates them—than it says about student achievement.

Grading practices also impact student behaviors. Teachers who believe that students are motivated by fear of punishment use grades as a threat to scare students. Conversely, teachers who believe that students thrive on encouragement use grades as feedback and as a form of recognition. Thus, grading practices can serve to either encourage or damage student motivation.

Turning from the classroom to the school level, the master schedule is to a school what grading practices are to teachers and classrooms. It reveals the true values and priorities of the school community. Examining the school's master schedule is like looking at an MRI of the inner workings of a school. It is the window to the school's soul.

How the master schedule is constructed may be as important as what the master schedule contains. For example, it provides insight into how professionals interact and how key decisions are made in the school. In addition, the process for developing the master schedule can either encourage or discourage staff members from providing input into scheduling decisions about individual students.

By this time, most schools have figured out what they want students to know and be able to do, and they have aligned their curriculum with state standards. In addition, most schools are either developing or have developed common formative assessments that help them decide if students are on track to learn these standards. However, the real test for the school comes when students are *not* learning. How does the school respond to students who are not succeeding or who need extra help? It is how the school responds to this question that determines whether it is focused on the needs and desires of the adults who work there or on the needs of the students who attend. The master schedule provides an important gauge of this staff vs. student balance.

In adult-focused schools, the master schedule reflects a world designed to address adult needs. There are few or no interventions, since offering these might make it more difficult to schedule students for required courses. All students are expected to complete courses in the same time frame. There are no double-block classes or flexible time frames for students to complete courses. The best, most experienced teachers are teaching the top students in AP or advanced classes, and the student-teacher ratio is often the lowest in these classes. Finally, in adult-focused schools, teachers with seniority are teaching only higher-level courses, no standard courses.

In student- or learning-focused schools, the master schedule reflects the needs of the students. There are multiple, tiered interventions. For example, instead of one reading intervention, there may be three or more. There are flexible time slots that allow students to progress at their own rates. Accommodations are built into the schedule for students who need math every day or who need three semesters to complete a science course. The best, most experienced teachers are teaching the neediest students. Teachers of higher-level courses also teach standard-level courses. Finally, the neediest students are in the smallest classes.

The process used to build the schedule is also different. The development of the master schedule in an adult-focused school is a closed process, often built by one person behind closed doors. Teachers and other staff members are asked to submit requests, but final decisions rest in the hands of one or a few people. It may be that staff members with an in get what they want. The others get the leftovers. In schools that are adult-focused, students are batch scheduled. All the individual requests are entered into the computer, and every student has the same chance as every other student to obtain their desired courses.

Conversely, the development of the master schedule in student-focused schools is an open process. Schools that are focused on student needs are set up to develop a customized learning plan for each student. Because mass customization is expensive in terms of time, effort, knowledge, expertise, and resources, the staff works collaboratively in teams specifically established to best meet the needs of each student and in ways that make effective use of school resources. The development of the master schedule is the result of the work of several teams throughout the school.

Teachers are most concerned with what they teach, then with where they teach, and, finally, when they teach. Therefore, instructional teams have the final say about who teaches what subjects. The where can be decided collaboratively across teams or departments. And the when—which involves putting the puzzle together—can be a team effort among the counselor, instructional leaders, and teachers or team leaders. Changes in any one of the inputs are only made with the consent of all involved parties.

In student- or learning-focused schools, individual schedules are constructed collaboratively. Math, science, world language, and social studies teachers meet with their colleagues in their respective disciplines and make course recommendations for specific students that are compiled and shared with counselors. The teachers of students with special needs—including students with disabilities and ELLs—act in an advisory capacity and work in concert with the counselor to hand-schedule these students.

Individual Learning Plan: Personalization Demands Collaboration

To ensure that we continue to have a significant number of students who fail, fall through the cracks, and drop out, all we have to do is do what we did in the past—teach the same lessons using the same methods in the same time frame. We can also perpetuate the same sorting and weeding-out process by scheduling all students in the same manner that we have always scheduled them. We fill out a form, put the form into the computer, and let the chips fall where they may. On the other hand, if we want each student to succeed, every student will need a customized, personal learning plan.

While expectations have risen sharply, schools and school counselors, at best, must do more with the same resources. The question then is how do we raise both the quantity and quality of what we do for students? How do we personalize the school and provide a customized plan for each student with no added resources?

As schools seek to meet student needs, the course offerings and master schedules of schools set up for student success have become more and more complex. There may be multiple reading interventions, several forms of algebra, and various recommended course sequences within various disciplines based on the readiness of the students. Students with weak literacy skills may be better off in certain science courses, while students with weak math skills but stronger literacy skills may be best placed in another science course.

Teachers often complain that students are improperly placed, and the first part of every school year is spent correcting scheduling problems. Unfortunately, the students most in need lose valuable learning time in this scenario and many never catch up. Thus, in reality, schools pay a steep price for correcting problems after the fact. If more time was devoted to scheduling up front, there would be no need to make corrections.

The solution to the problem of properly scheduling students and providing personalized learning plans for each student is to make better use of the resources that we already have. Instead of the math, science, or world language teachers complaining, they need to be directly involved in scheduling every student. This is more than passing on individual recommendations on a form. Subject-area teachers need to take the time to meet, collaborate, and decide on the best recommendation for each student.

Personalization demands such collaboration. The same people working with the same number of students in the same allotted time in the same way will get the same results. It is unrealistic to expect that one person (the counselor) will have the knowledge, expertise, and sophistication needed to provide a customized plan for every student in an increasingly complicated and complex instructional setting.

The old silos must come down. School staff members need to give up the notion that this is my job and that is your job (i.e., teaching is my job and scheduling students is your job). Student success is the shared responsibility of every staff member. The need to provide both access and excellence for every student and the complexity of the curriculum needed to do so means that we need input from professionals with specialized expertise in their field. School counselors can no longer rely on checklists to schedule students, and teachers can no longer afford to remain detached from the scheduling and planning process.

The construction of a personalized learning plan must begin with the person who is the best qualified person to make specific recommendations—the classroom teacher. Subject-area teachers should analyze the performance of each student in their respective subjects and make recommendations for the next most appropriate course in the sequence. In other words, the specialists in each field should recommend a treatment plan in their area of expertise. Math teachers recommend math courses, science teachers recommend science courses, and so on. These recommendations are then passed on to the counselor and adviser.

A Differentiated, Multi-Tiered Approach to Personalized Planning

The following multi-tiered approach to constructing personal learning plans follows a simple but logical approach. More staff members are involved in the construction of the personalized learning plan of those students most in need, and the counselor assumes the role of a team leader who facilitates the development of each student plan.

Level I Plan—Most secondary schools today help students develop an overall graduation plan that contains a sequence of math, science, social studies, English, world language, and career and technical education elective courses. This plan is sufficient for a significant portion of a school's population. The Level I Plan is constructed by the counselor after the following:

1. Diagnostic data are collected and analyzed.

2. Performance data, including grades and state and national test results, are collected.

3. Teachers in each department meet, collaborate, and make placement recommendations.

4. Counselor meets with each student and finalizes the personal learning plan.

Level II Plan—Certain students are known to have specific learning needs. ELLs, students with disabilities, and others with specific, identified learning needs should have staff advisers who work with the student and counselor to form a plan. This ensures that these students are placed in courses that provide flexible time allotments, appropriate settings, and required resources. The Level II plan requires that the following steps take place:

1. Diagnostic data are collected and analyzed.

2. Performance data, including grades and state and national test results, are collected.

3. Teachers in each department meet, collaborate, and make recommendations.

4. Teacher-advisor reviews recommendations, compares the recommendations with existing plans (e.g., IEP), and makes recommendations.

5. Counselor meets with teacher-advisor, reviews recommendations, and finalizes the plan.

6. Counselor and teacher-advisor meet with the student and finalize the personal learning plan.

Level III Plan—Some students will need targeted interventions, which will require a high level of specific knowledge and additional inputs from experts in specific academic areas. For example, a student's diagnostic reading assessment indicates that the student is sufficiently below target that he may need a reading intervention. In this case, the literacy coach or reading specialist should make the placement recommendation. The Level III Plan is constructed as follows:

1. Diagnostic data are collected and analyzed.

2. Performance data, including grades and state and national test results, are collected.

3. Teachers in each department meet, collaborate, and make recommendations.

4. Specialist reviews diagnostic data and makes recommendation.

5. Teacher-advisor reviews recommendations, compares the recommendations with already existing plans (e.g., IEP), and makes recommendation.

6. Counselor meets with teacher-advisor and learning specialist to review recommendations and finalize the plan.

7. Counselor and teacher-advisor meet with the student and finalize the personal learning plan.

The current reality is such that any young adult who does not possess the skills that make them college-, career-, and workplace-ready will effectively be sentenced to a lifetime of marginal employment and second-class citizenship. We must create schools in which every student graduates and where every graduate is college-, career-, and workplace-ready.

This daunting task will require that schools transform themselves from a 20th-century, teacher-focused, factory model that sorts students for success to a 21st-century, student-focused, customized model in which every student receives an individualized approach. Not only must we adapt and change the "old school" structures and processes, we must change the way we work. The old, top-down, centralized school will give way to a flatter, less hierarchical, more collaborative learning environment where leadership is shared and distributed throughout.

The complexity of today's schools demands that we work closely together to ensure that we leave no stone unturned in our efforts to educate our students. Principals and counselors must work in a collaborative partnership with the entire staff focusing all available resources toward providing each and every student a customized place that offers the best possible chance of success.

Reference

ACT. (2008). *The forgotten middle: Ensuring that all students are on target for college and career readiness before high school.* Retrieved from http://www.act.org/research/policymakers/reports/ForgottenMiddle.html

Chapter 2
Principal-Counselor Alliance for Accountability and Data Use

Carolyn B. Stone and Carol Dahir

"Without data you don't know where you are, you don't know where you are going, and you don't know if you ever got there."

—Jim MacGregor, High School Counselor
(University of North Florida & Stone, 2006)

School counselors and principals share responsibility and accountability for students. This has been a driving force in the national effort to transform the work of school counselors. A new paradigm has emerged in which school counselors and principals find themselves in a powerful alliance to support the accountability imperative of the No Child Left Behind Act (NCLB; U.S. Department of Education, 2002). Data use is a critically important tool in school efforts to make progress toward goals against which they will be measured.

Carolyn B. Stone is a Professor of Counselor Education at University of North Florida. Email cstone@unf.edu. Carol Dahir is an Associate Professor of Counselor Education at New York Institute of Technology. Email cdahir@nyit.edu.

As the role of data and accountability has changed over the last 6 decades, principals have grown the ranks of school counselors (Bauman et al., 2003; U. S. Department of Labor, Bureau of Labor Statistics, 2008). The growth was instigated because principals value their skills as counselors, collaborators, and coordinators of student services (Myrick, 2002).

With the advent of NCLB and other critical educational policies, school improvement efforts have been accompanied by the forging of a new alliance between counselors and principals. The historical focus on the specialized skills of school counselors that initially garnered principal support and increased counseling positions has shifted to the question of how counselors' unique skills impact student achievement and school improvement goals. As a direct result of the principal/counselor alliance, the fundamental question of "what do school counselors do" has changed to "how are students different because of the school counseling program in their school."

NCLB accountability mandates have changed the role of the building-level school principal and, concurrently, all educators under the school house roof, requiring all to demonstrate the value they add to raising student achievement (National Commission on Excellence in Education, 1983; U.S. Department of Education, 2001; U.S. House of Representatives, 1984). The recent inclusion of school counselor accountability in the American School Counselor Association (ASCA) National Model (See Appendix A) and in subsequent state iterations parallels such changes and was a worthy transformation of the profession.

Shared Leadership for Accountability

School counselors can contribute their leadership skills and join forces with principals and other key stakeholders to impact student success. The last 10 years has seen the traditional service delivery model replaced with a decidedly higher profile role involving improving student achievement. The Education Trust, with the financial support of the Wallace-Reader's Digest Fund, furthered the conversations around school counselors' impact on the achievement gap. The Transforming School Counseling Initiative (TSCI) was developed to change school counselor preparation and practice so that school counselors would become more instrumental in helping to close the achievement gap between poor and minority youth and their more advantaged peers (Education Trust, 2007).

Principals and district level administrators are redefining their allies in the high stakes accountability world and moving toward collaborative leadership to accomplish the difficulties of moving student data elements (Barton, 2005).

Exploring the potential for the school counselor/principal partnership would take this entire book and in no way exhaust the possibilities. This chapter focuses on a few of the powerful ways the school counselor/principal partnership can impact student achievement through collaborative data use and shared accountability that influences:

1. Equity and the achievement gap;
2. System barriers;
3. Student aspirations and course enrollment patterns;
4. Resource brokering; and
5. The instructional program.

Equity and the achievement gap. Equity is still dependent in large part on a student's socioeconomic status. Students from low-socioeconomic families are accessing rigor at a much reduced rate than that of their more affluent counterparts (Education Trust, 2006). To compound the problem, students who need the most are traditionally given the least when they get to school (Haycock, 2007).

By disaggregating student data, principals and counselors can identify student groups being left out of the success equation and the practices that may be deterring equity of opportunity. Principals and school counselors who understand equity issues can carefully analyze course enrollment pattern data to determine which students are not included in rigorous academics. Together, through leadership and advocacy, school practices that may be deterring equitable access and opportunities for student success in higher-level academics can be eliminated. Review of student databases reveal patterns of stratification of opportunity for certain races, genders, zip codes, and school assignments.

> By containing the data in this type of program, assurances are built into the system that no students are left out of the picture when viewing the data. This provides equity in analysis as well as in access to opportunities, and also guarantees that no group of students will be left out of calculations. (Stone & Turba, 1999, para. 12)

These issues resonate with counselors, and not simply from the perspective of accountability for the sake of quantifying school counseling program outcomes. The promise of a brighter future for all students, especially those who languish in the achievement gap, stirs the social justice conscience in school counselors and propels them toward action. Hart and Jacobi (1992) were instrumental in starting the conversations about the need for school counselors to work to close the achievement gap and serve both as leaders and advocates for change.

System barriers. School counselors, who analyze data to ferret out stratification of student opportunity, are positioned as significant systemic change agents. Using school district data, the principal/counselor team can identify systemwide practices that contribute to inequitable situations for individual students (Stone & Turba, 1999, p. 5). Together, they can work to manage and monitor patterns of enrollment and student success.

Darvin Boothe, principal of Lake Butler High School in central Florida, arrived at his high school approximately 28 years ago and found that admissions into higher-level academics mirrored most high schools of the time. Lake Butler had a very regulated approach to admissions into rigorous academics. For example, for most Advanced Placement (AP) courses, students had to have a 3.0 GPA, B or better in prior coursework, 55+ on Verbal PSAT, 550+ on Verbal SAT, and instructor's approval. Thus, it was not surprising that, in 1981, only 36 students enrolled in AP courses, with students taking 55 AP exams and 22 of them scoring a 3 or better. Mr. Boothe set about making changes in the admissions policy for higher-level courses, largely as a result of soul searching after intervening to get his own son into AP courses. His son did very well in AP, and Mr. Boothe began to worry. What about all those other students who did not have the advantage of having an advocate? His determination to open more doors for students to access higher-level academics yielded sizable results. Mr. Boothe, collaborating with his school counseling department, started pushing for more access into rigorous coursework. Steadily, progress was made. In 1998, 358 Lake Butler students took 765 exams and scored 3 or better on 409 exams, and, in 2006, an impressive 853 students took 1,922 exams, with a score of 3 or better on 872 of those exams. This powerful principal/school counselor partnership has advantaged thousands of students (Stone, 2006).

Student aspirations and course enrollment patterns. School counselors have the ethical imperative to positively impact students' desire to stretch and strive academically by helping them understand their choices and the full weight and meaning of those choices (American School Counselor Association, 2004; Stone & Turba, 1999). Career advising helps to close the information gap by helping students see the interrelatedness of the curriculum and the consequences of academic choices. Closing the information gap helps students understand that their chosen course enrollment actually widens, or narrows, future economic possibilities (Noguera & Wing, 2006).

> Brighter futures, especially for poor and minority students, are almost inextricably connected to the course of study they follow in school. The lack of proactive, focused guidance to get students into the right curriculum and support them once there can be a huge barrier, preventing them from participating unconditionally in the 21st Century economy. (Martin, House, & Robinson, 2000, p. 1)

Principals and district level administrators are redefining their allies in the high stakes accountability world and moving toward collaborative leadership to accomplish the difficulties of moving student data elements (Barton, 2005).

Raising aspirations of students includes but is not limited to:

1. Raising students' awareness and understanding of career and academic options available to them;

2. Helping students and their families learn about the interrelatedness among career options, academic options, postsecondary education, and future economic opportunities;

3. Helping students and their families understand which courses a student should take to prepare for the widest opportunities after high school;

4. Helping students and families understand and complete postsecondary admission processes and financial aid procedures while allowing them access to information about the costs of a higher education and strategies to pay for it; and

5. Increasing the number of students enrolling in rigorous coursework that will satisfy college admission requirements.

Resource brokering. To significantly extend their reach to more students, counselors and principals need to collaborate to more effectively manage resources. An example of school counselors taking a leadership role in brokering resources to reach all students can be found in high schools in Jacksonville, Florida, where each individual student is informed of available financial aid and scholarship opportunities. The school counselors collaborate annually with their principals and the guidance supervisor to train and place approximately 100 volunteers into the district's 17 high schools. The volunteers deliver individual advising sessions on accessing financial aid and scholarships for postsecondary education. Harvey Harper has been volunteering each year in the program since its inception in 1991 and represents the commitment of the community that has helped countless students have greater hope for financing a postsecondary education. A similar program called Horizons is conducted during students' junior year but includes more detailed information on college entrance examinations. When students understand that financing higher education is possible, they can have hope and be inspired to do better in school (Stone, 2003).

Instructional program. While principals are seen as instructional leaders in their school, counselors need to be role models and change agents, which is more easily accomplished when they are seen in a leadership role in the schools. The more they are in the classrooms and working with teachers, parents, and administrators, the more credible they become (Clark & Stone, 2000; Guerra 1998; Hart & Jacobi, 1992).

Through the collaborative efforts of the school counselor, principal, and other key stakeholders, the instructional program can be strengthened. Conducting staff development for teachers and parents in such important areas as educational planning, motivation, student appraisal, interventions, and diversity issues are a few examples of how school counselors play a unique role in fostering understanding and cooperation within the school community. Student leadership training, cooperative discipline, classroom management, study skills, and college admissions procedures are areas that have long been used by school counselors to impact the instructional program. The opportunities are limitless and, through skillful collaboration with teachers, school counselors can consider it a serious responsibility to impact instruction by providing information, support, student interventions, usable achievement data, learning strategies, and encouragement (Stone, 2003).

Impacting the instructional program is just what Bernadette Willette, a counselor in rural Maine, was able to accomplish through data analysis and advocacy. Her high school, a low-socioeconomic school, did not have any AP courses. Bernadette reached out to College Board for help, and they provided her with evidence showing a correlation between the PSAT scores of students and students' predicted success in AP courses. Armed with hard evidence that the students of the school could be successful in AP courses and, therefore, have greater opportunities in higher education, Bernadette shared the facts with her teachers. When the teachers learned that many of their students' PSAT scores predicted success in AP courses and realized that, without change, these students would graduate without having the opportunity to take those courses, the teachers made the commitment to offer AP courses in the future. Bernadette wrote a grant to support the teacher training needed, and now five AP courses are offered at this tiny high school at the end of the Interstate 95 system. Bernadette, with the support and collaboration of the administration of her school, changed the instructional program and widened opportunities for many students.

Data-Driven Decision Making

Data only take on value when used to inform decisions. Two types of data are available to principals and school counselors—qualitative (e.g., perception and process) and quantitative (e.g., test scores, discipline referrals, retention rates, course enrollment, and attendance). These data can be used to assess the impact of the counseling program on improving practices and student outcomes.

Perception data allow you to analyze changes in attitudes, beliefs, or needs over time and are often collected as pre- and post-information, needs assessments, or surveys. Data from these examples can also provide "moment in time" or "snapshot" data.

Process data provide important evidence that the event occurred and information about how the activity was conducted. Process data measure implementation of programs and the amount of time school counselors are engaged in a particular activity such as individual counseling. For example, school counselors may present the numbers of students seen individually, in groups, or in classrooms (Stone & Dahir, 2007). Another example of process data is the program audit, which establishes the degree of implementation of a comprehensive school counseling program, identifies areas for improvement, and provides an overall view of the total program effectiveness. It offers another piece of information that can contribute to program success (Stone & Dahir, 2007).

Impact data provide information to evaluate programs. Generally the data support or do not support the goals of the program. For example, if a counseling office stated as its goal *to increase the number of applications submitted by seniors*, then the impact data would be the total number of applications submitted by seniors or the mean number of applications submitted by seniors. Another example might be that a middle school with a goal of *improving the school climate of safety* would use perception data from students about how safe they felt when at school.

Critical Data Elements

During the school improvement process, stakeholders must identify what measures will indicate success. These are the critical data elements that can be used to answer the question of how the school is making a difference. These data need to include traditional student achievement data, such as attendance, graduation rates, postsecondary planning rates, and standardized testing, as well as impact data like the number of students with completed college applications. By using school-based data, school counselors can make informed decisions about ways to improve student outcomes.

Any number of methods can be used to generate data, from sophisticated student information management (SIM) technology to the more simplified approach of hand counting. For example, if the number of student absences is the critical data element that the principal and school counselor are trying to affect, then the SIM technology could be queried and disaggregated in a number of different ways (e.g., days of the week students are absent, ethnicity, grade level, etc.) or teachers can simply keep a list of students in their classes whose absences fall within the parameters established. The method selected must be appropriate to the objective or goal and should be attainable without investing too much time in the data collection piece. Data can also be generated from district, state, or federal information reports.

Conclusions

Principals and counselors across America are teaming in strategically important ways, such as those highlighted in this chapter. When the principal and school counselor think of themselves as allies and routinely collaborate, they are maximizing their opportunity to effectively promote the academic success for all the students in their charge. Emphasis on the critical data elements (e.g., grades, course enrollment patterns, dropout rates, test scores, retention rates, and attendance rates) should be a powerful focus of the principal/school counselor alliance. When counselors and principals begin with data specific to their school and identify areas which need improvement, they can also identify the logical point for building a developmental counseling program which helps to address those needs (Stone & Dahir, 2007).

Principals are joining forces with other educators to assume and exert leadership within their schools and communities. School counselors are poised to be part of this leadership effort, helping to establish a vision and belief in the development of high aspirations for every child. Opportunities for collaborative leadership are plentiful. The accountability measures of NCLB require principals to widen their circle of leadership to be more distributive (inclusive) so that the systematic collection, analysis, and use of data informs every educator's practice, especially that of the school counselor.

Questions for Reflection

Principals, use the following questions for reflection:

1. Data-driven school counseling is still new to many schools. Am I willing to start the conversations about the need for all educators, including the school counselors, to use data to decide how to best impact student outcomes?

2. What data can the school counselor(s) and I collaborate on this school year to positively impact student success?

3. How will my school counseling faculty need to be supported to implement the strategies to move this critical data in a positive direction? Will they need professional development in data use? Resources? A shifting of duties to reallocate time?

4. Am I willing to evaluate my school counseling faculty on the same critical student data outcomes on which I am evaluated? If not, why not?

5. Do I have a school counselor's voice on my leadership team?

References

American School Counselor Association. (2004). *Ethical standards for school counselors*. Alexandria, VA: Author.

Barton, R. (2005). Collaborating to reach NCLB goals. *Research Brief, 11*(1). Retrieved September 9, 2008, from http://www.nwrel.org/nwedu/ 11-01/brief/

Bauman, S., Siegel, J., Falco, L., Szymanski, G., Davis, A., & Seabolt, K. (2003). Trends in school counseling journals: The first fifty years. *Professional School Counseling, 7*(2), 79-90.

Clark, M., & Stone, C. (2000). Evolving our image: School counselors as educational leaders. In J. Wittmer & M. A. Clark, *Managing your school guidance and counseling program K-12 developmental strategies* (pp. 75-82). Minneapolis, MN: Educational Media Corp.

Education Trust. (2006). *Key education facts and figures: Achievement, attainment and opportunity from elementary school through college.* Retrieved from http://www2.edtrust.org/edtrust/summaries2006/USA.pdf

Education Trust. (2007). *Background for transforming school counselor preparation.* Retrieved September 4, 2008, from http://www2.edtrust.org/EdTrust/ Transforming+School+Counseling/background.htm

Guerra, P. (1998, April). Reaction to DeWitt Wallace grant overwhelming. *Counseling Today, 13.*

Hart, P., & Jacobi, M. (1992). *From gatekeeper to advocate: Transforming the role of the school counselor.* New York: College Entrance Examination Board.

Haycock, K. (2007). *Written testimony of Kati Haycock, President of The Education Trust, on the teacher quality provisions of No Child Left Behind.* Retrieved September 2, 2008, from http://www2.edtrust.org/EdTrust/Press+Room/ TitleIITestimony.htm

Martin, P., House, R., & Robinson, S. (2000). *Metropolitan Life Foundation National School Counselor Training Initiative: Professional development for practice in 21st century schools.* Unpublished grant application.

Myrick, R. (2002). *Developmental guidance and counseling: A practical approach* (4th ed.). Minneapolis, MN: Educational Media Corporation.

National Commission on Excellence in Education. (1983). *A nation at risk.* Washington, DC: U.S. Department of Education.

Noguera, P. A., & Wing, J. Y. (Eds.). (2006). *Unfinished business: Closing the racial achievement gap in our schools.* San Francisco, CA: Jossey-Bass.

Stone, C. (2003, April). The new school counselor: Agent of change. *The College Board Review, 199,* 45-48.

Stone, C. (2006). Ethical behavior and high school reform. *The Voice of the School Counselor, 17*(1), 1-3. Retrieved September 2, 2008, from http://www.txca. org/images/tca/tsca/AugnewsPROOF.pdf

Stone, C., & Dahir, C. (2007). *School counselor accountability: A measure of student success* (2nd ed.). Upper Saddle River, NJ: Pearson Education, Inc.

Stone, C., & Turba, R. (1999). School counselors using technology for advocacy. *The Journal of Technology in Counseling, 1*(1). Retrieved from http://jtc. colstate.edu/vol1_1/advocacy.htm

University of North Florida (Producer), & Stone, C. (Director). (2006). *A pioneer in data-driven school counseling* [Motion picture].

U.S. Department of Education. (2002). No Child Left Behind Act of 2001 (H.R.1). Washington, DC: Author.

U. S. Department of Labor, Bureau of Labor Statistics. (2008). *Counselors.* Washington, DC: Author. Retrieved September 9, 2008, from http://www. bls.gov/oco/ocos067.htm

U.S. House of Representatives. (1984). National Science Foundation Authorization. *Hearings before the Subcommittee on Science, Research and Technology of the Committee on Science and Technology, Washington, DC, 43.*

Chapter 3

School Counselors and Principals Partnering for Achievement: What Does the Research Evidence Say?

Carey Dimmitt, Matt Militello, and Chris Janson

Today's educational landscape is characterized by complex challenges. Foremost of these challenges is the question of how to improve student achievement. Principals are being held increasingly accountable for outcomes in the buildings they lead, and school counselors are expected to demonstrate their impact on student achievement as well. Any decision made by a principal or school counselor (e.g., which curriculum to implement, students to talk to, teachers to consult, data to analyze, etc.) has the potential to impact the achievement outcomes of the school. Knowing what works helps us to make informed decisions about which interventions, programs,

Carey Dimmitt, Ph.D., is the Associate Director of the Center for School Counseling Outcome Research, and an Associate Professor and the Coordinator of the School Counseling Program at the University of Massachusetts, Amherst. Email cdimmitt@educ.umass.edu. Matt Militello, Ph.D., is an Assistant Professor of Educational Leadership and Policy Studies at North Carolina State University. Email matt_militello@ncsu.edu. Chris Janson, Ph.D., is an Assistant Professor in the Department of Leadership, Counseling, and Instructional Technology at the University of North Florida. Email c.janson@unf.edu.

and models are most likely to be successful, and is an important way to ensure that we are on the right track to increasing student learning. Doing what we know works, whether through research, site-specific evaluation, or established practice, is the basis of effective education and, hence, of student achievement.

Every day, school professionals are engaged in work that is making a difference. Evaluating those methods and practices and then sharing the results is what is needed to attain large-scale progress. In this chapter, we will review what is currently known about effective practices for both principals and school counselors, and we will make suggestions for the practical application of relevant research. Since principals and school counselors will all be more successful when there are effective partnerships, we will present models for this kind of collaboration as well.

What Works?
- Effective leadership
- Quality curriculum and instruction
- Effective school counseling programs and interventions
- Collaboration

School Principals and Achievement

Leadership matters. Leadership of the principal is "second only to classroom instruction among all school-related factors that contribute to what students learn at school" (Leithwood, Seashore Louis, Anderson, & Wahlstrom, 2004, p. 7). What do we know about school leadership practices that work? Effective school leaders have crucial and specific skills and knowledge, which are summarized in Table 3.1.

Table 3.1. Skills and Knowledge of Effective School Leaders	
Management skills	• Articulate a vision • Foster acceptance of group goals • Create high performance expectations • Support staff development • Encourage organizational redesign
Pedagogical expertise	• Endorse more powerful forms of teaching • Promote student learning
Community-building skills	• Create strong communities of students, teachers, and parents • Nurture educational cultures among families

Source: Militello, Rallis, & Goldring, 2009

In addition, we know that the school principal is uniquely positioned to shape a school's culture (Deal & Peterson, 1998). Specifically, the principal of a school can have great influence on the school structures and on the relationships and learning that exist in the organization. In fact, Hallinger and Heck (1996) report that school leadership, through interactions with teachers, accounts for one quarter to one third of the total school effect on student achievement. What we also know is that the greatest impact on student achievement *inside the school walls* is teaching. Combining these factors synthesizes what effective principals look like; successful principals lead meaningful and proficient professional learning communities (see Figure 3.1) that support the critical work of teachers.

Figure 3.1. Principal Leadership of Professional Learning Communities

Organizational Impact

Focus on
Teaching and Learning

Professional Learning Community

Professional Learning Communities

What are professional learning communities? Wenger (1999) explains that "practice is the source of coherence of a community" (p. 73), and this coherence is manifested in a community as three basic characteristics: *joint enterprise, mutual engagement,* and a *shared repertoire* (see Figure 3.2). Wenger (1999) defines *joint enterprise* as the meaning or understanding that the members of a community have negotiated regarding what they will mutually accomplish. *Mutual engagement* requires that members of the community interact with one another regularly to develop new skills, refine old ones, and incorporate new ways of understanding the shared enterprise (Wenger, 1999). In a community of practice, *shared repertoire* is the "communal resources that members have developed over time through their mutual engagement" (Wenger, 1999, p. 4). This shared repertoire may consist of artifacts, documents, language, vocabulary, routines, technology, etc. Research has indicated that when principals lead efforts to create such communities, improvements in student achievement can be seen (Marks & Printy, 2003; Printy, 2008).

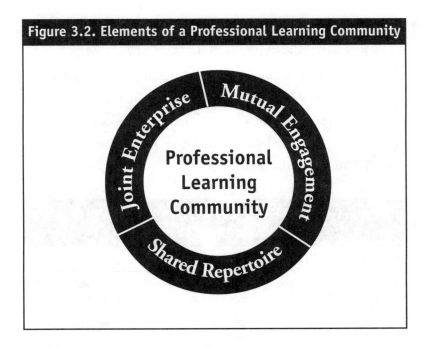

Figure 3.2. Elements of a Professional Learning Community

Principal Leadership to Innovate and Implement a Professional Learning Community

Specific leadership behaviors in schools and their impact on student learning have been a long-term topic of educational research. Marzano, Waters, and McNulty (2005) looked at a number of studies examining principal leadership behaviors and conducted a meta-analysis using only empirical research. They found that specific principal leadership behaviors that generated second-order changes consistently led to student achievement improvements, and they define second-order change as consisting of broad and substantive shifts in attitudes and beliefs which cause significant behavioral change. Such change usually indicates a considerable break from past practices and requires education and leadership to be effective (Marzano et al., 2005). This type of change has also been called transformative (Burns, 1978; Moore-Johnson, 1996) or adaptive

(Heifetz & Linsky, 2002). In their meta-analysis, Marzano et al., found that, of 21 principal "responsibilities," "situational awareness" (i.e., the ability to be aware of the details and undercurrents of the school) was most highly correlated with student academic achievement. However, seven others were found to be most important to the principal's ability to lead second-order change efforts in a school. Table 3.2 highlights these seven behaviors.

Table 3.2. Principal Behaviors Positively Associated With Second-Order Change	
Behavior	**Definition**
Knowledge of Curriculum, Instruction, & Assessment	Is knowledgeable about current curriculum, instruction, and assessment practices.
Optimizer	Inspires and leads new and challenging innovations.
Intellectual Stimulation	Ensures that faculty and staff are aware of the most current theories and practices and makes the discussion of these a regular aspect of the school's culture.
Change Agent	Is willing to and does actively challenge the status quo.
Monitors/Evaluates	Monitors the effectiveness of school practices and their impact on student learning.
Flexibility	Adapts his or her leadership behavior to the needs of the current situation and is comfortable with dissent.
Ideals/Beliefs	Communicates and operates from strong ideals and beliefs about schooling.

Source: Marzano et al., 2005

In another large-scale meta-analysis of school leadership literature, the Stanford Educational Leadership Institute (Darling-Hammond, LaPointe, Meyerson, & Orr, 2007) found that effective principals:

- Develop deep understandings of how to *support teachers;*

- Manage the *curriculum* to promote student learning; and

- Transform schools into effective organizations that *build capacity for teachers* to promote student learning for all students.

Both meta-analyses provide evidence of what knowledge, skills, and dispositions school principals need to have to support systemic changes. These studies also reiterate the importance of focusing on teaching and learning, making it clear that principals must fully understand the multiple components and dimensions of teaching and learning, and that faculty must engage in meaningful professional development and pedagogical practices. The most successful principals provide "intellectual leadership for growth in teaching skill" (Resnick & Glennan, 2002, p. 160), in addition to opportunities for professional development.

Principals cannot simply expect teachers and other staff to engage in new actions without structures, supports, and resources. According to Newman, King, and Young (2000), the development of a school's capacity must include not only the development of knowledge, skills, and dispositions of individuals but also (1) the existence of a functional problem-solving professional learning community,

(2) schoolwide program coherence, and (3) availability and accessibility of technical resources to support teacher and student work. Principals can create the organizational coherence needed to provide a stable platform to develop individual capacity and teacher-leaders, advocate for appropriate resources, implement support mechanisms, and focus the entire school community on student learning. Even with dynamic and effective individual capacity building, a dysfunctional organization can hinder any reform effort—regardless of the stakes (Elmore, 2003, 2004). As a result, developing and sustaining a professional learning community takes capacity *and* coherence.

What Works?
- Individual skill development
- Professional learning communities
- Organizational coherence
- Technical resources
- Focus on student learning

School Counselors and Student Achievement

School counselors are also uniquely positioned to impact student achievement because they are often at the center of data flow involving students, and because school counselor training prepares them with skills and knowledge about the broader educational issues that influence schools and the students within them (Clark & Stone,

2000; Kern, 1999). The broad academic preparation of school counselors includes counseling, learning theories, program evaluation, child development, family systems, testing, special education, career development, consultation, and so on. This knowledge base can make counselors "natural leaders" in schools (Borders & Shoffner, 2003, pp. 52-53), but requires both active engagement in school activities outside the guidance office on the part of school counselors and active support of and collaboration with the school principal.

School counselors are both mental health practitioners and educators (American School Counselors Association [ASCA], 2005). In order to most effectively impact student achievement, school counselors need to utilize research in both domains, and this combination of information creates an optimal situation to impact student outcomes, advocate for student achievement, and act as leaders in the efforts to close achievement gaps (ASCA, 2005; Dimmitt, Carey, & Hatch, 2007; House & Hayes, 2002; House & Martin, 1998). Reviews of research in this area repeatedly identify the challenges of conducting effective research in school counseling, the scarcity of relevant studies, and the need for more studies, but also consistently indicate that most school counseling interventions have a positive impact on a wide variety of key student outcomes, including student achievement (Borders & Drury, 1992; McGannon, Carey, & Dimmitt, 2006; Whiston & Sexton, 1998). Table 3.3 summarizes the meta-analyses and research summaries in the profession.

Table 3.3. Meta-Analyses and Research Summaries in School Counseling

Casey & Berman (1985)	Meta-analysis of research about the impact of individual counseling found that it can positively impact achievement, among other outcomes.
Eder & Whiston (2006)	Meta-analysis of research about psychotherapy with children and adolescents indicated that oppositional defiant disorder and conduct disorder were most effectively remediated with functional family therapy, multisystemic therapy, and/or parent management training. Attention deficit hyperactivity disorder can be positively impacted by parent management training. Anxiety, fear, and phobias in children and adolescents are most effectively treated through systematic desensitization, modeling, reinforced practice, and cognitive behavior therapy. Depressive symptoms are most effectively treated through cognitive-behavioral therapy.
Gerler (1985)	Reviewed school counseling interventions at the elementary school level with a focus on teacher consultations, counseling, and classroom guidance interventions. Found that classroom guidance was related to improvement in elementary school students' behaviors.
Hoag & Burlingame (1997)	Conducted a meta-analytic review of 49 studies about group counseling. Determined that group counseling interventions can have a moderate impact on academic achievement factors (Effect Size [ES] = .51).
Prout & DeMartino (1986)	Meta-analysis found that individual counseling impacted grade point average (ES = .58) and cognitive abilities (ES = .66).
Prout & Prout (1998)	Conducted a meta-analysis of counseling and psychotherapy in school settings, and concluded that there was strong evidence that these interventions are effective in this context (ES = .97).
Whiston & Sexton (1998)	Summarized 50 outcome studies published between 1988 and 1995 and found research support for interventions in the areas of career planning, group counseling, social skill training, and peer counseling.
Wilson (1986)	Focused on interventions with low-achieving students and their parents to determine whether school counseling interventions were effective in boosting academic achievement as measured by grade point average. Summary information suggested that counseling interventions can have positive effects on academic achievement with this population.

Comprehensive Developmental Guidance Programs

As with principals, many ways that school counselors impact student achievement are through the larger school context. The American School Counselor Association (ASCA) has developed the ASCA National Model (see Appendix A) for School Counseling Programs as a guide for this kind of schoolwide programming (ASCA, 2005). Studies that have measured the impact of school counseling at the program level have found that students are more successful in a number of domains when there is a Comprehensive Developmental Guidance (CDG) program in place.

In the strongest research to date, 150 public elementary schools in Washington state were randomly selected to participate in a study of the impact of elementary school counseling programs, with school and student diversity that was representative of the state in general. Schools with a CDG program, even if not fully implemented, were found to have higher scores on both norm-referenced national tests of academic knowledge and on state criterion-referenced tests of academic achievement (Sink & Stroh, 2003). Additionally, students who remained in the same school with a well-implemented CDG program for multiple years obtained higher achievement test scores than students who attended schools without such programs. Thus, more exposure to CDG programs was correlated with greater improvements in scores (Sink & Stroh, 2003).

Gysbers and Lapan and their colleagues in Missouri conducted two additional statewide studies of the effects of implementing CDG Programs (Lapan, Gysbers, & Petroski, 2001; Lapan, Gysbers, &

Sun, 1997). They found that, in middle and high schools with more fully implemented CDG programs, students report earning higher grades, having better relationships with teachers, and feeling greater satisfaction with school. Students in these schools were also more likely to report that education is relevant to later life, school is safe, and, at the high school level, that career and college information is accessible.

Though these results are promising, the findings are correlational rather than causal. The positive outcomes could be due to factors in addition to the implementation of the CDG program, such as other educational programs that impact academic achievement. For example, more complete guidance implementation and student achievement might both result from the schools' organizational structure, leadership, and/or personnel strengths rather than being causally related to each other. In all likelihood, given the complexity of both human behavior and educational outcomes, many interacting factors are responsible for the findings, including—but not limited to—the school counseling programs.

What Works?
- Comprehensive Developmental Guidance programs
- Schoolwide interventions
- Positive Behavioral Supports (PBS)
- Peer counseling and tutoring
- PeaceBuilders program
- BullyBusters program

Schoolwide Interventions

Schoolwide interventions designed to develop the skills that students need to succeed are widely implemented by school counselors—often in collaboration with multiple school colleagues—and usually with generally successful outcomes. An example is the PeaceBuilders program, which was designed to improve school environments and learning by reducing aggressive behavior and increasing social competence. Designed for use with students in grades K-5, the program includes classroom curriculum, schoolwide implementation of guidelines for social interactions, and teacher training in reinforcing positive behaviors. Other schoolwide programs with good research support for their effectiveness are BullyBusters, Positive Behavioral Support, and peer counseling and tutoring (see Table 3.4). An excellent resource in this area is the What Works Clearinghouse (U.S. Department of Education, 2009), which identifies research-based interventions in education.

Guidance Curriculum

The guidance curriculum is an efficient and effective way for school counselors to impact student achievement. Reviews of school counseling outcome research have consistently found that school counseling curriculum interventions concerning career, academic, and social/personal development can positively impact student knowledge in each of those domains (Dimmitt et al., 2007). Table 3.5 summarizes this data.

Table 3.4. Schoolwide Interventions	
Embry, Flannery, Vazsonyi, Powell, & Atha (1996); Flannery et al. (2003); Vazsonyi, Bellison, & Flannery (2004)	The PeaceBuilders program focuses on increasing socially responsive behaviors and on reducing aggressive behavior with K-5 students. Studies have found increases in prosocial behavior and decreases in teacher-reported aggressive behavior, with greater impact for those who were initially lower in skills at the beginning of the study.
Luiselli, Putnam, Handler, & Feinberg (2005); Nelson, Martella, & Marchand-Martella (2002)	Positive Behavioral Support (PBS) is a schoolwide process for improving student behaviors and academic outcomes with strong research support.
Newman-Carlson & Horne (2004)	Research indicates that teachers' self-reported ability to manage problematic behaviors before escalation improved as a result of the BullyBusters intervention, and that related disciplinary referrals and classroom management problems decreased. This intervention was designed to change teacher knowledge and behavior rather than focusing on students.
Carty, Rosenbaum, Lafreniere, & Sutton (2000)	Completed a 4-year longitudinal study of schoolwide programs of peer counseling and the effects on adolescent development. Their findings indicated that students who received peer counseling services scored significantly higher on coping and social skills scales.

The curriculum intervention with the strongest research support to date is Student Success Skills, which focuses on cognitive, social, and self-management skills. Students who engage in this intervention have shown significantly stronger math and reading scores on a Florida state criterion-referenced academic test, the Florida Comprehensive Assessment Test (FCAT), with stronger results for those students who were initially scoring between the 25th and 50th percentile (Brigman & Campbell, 2003; Brigman & Webb, 2004; Brigman, Webb, & Campbell, 2007).

What Works?
- Structured guidance curriculum
- Student Success Skills
- Second Step Violence Prevention curriculum
- Succeeding in School
- Curriculum topics
  - Anxiety reduction
  - Test-taking strategies
  - Goal setting
  - Problem solving
  - Career development

At the high school level, a guidance curriculum designed to educate students about goal setting, problem solving, career exploration, and school resources for students has been found to significantly improve student behavior, attitude, and knowledge in these areas (Schlossberg, Morris, & Lieberman, 2001). Guidance lessons about stress reduction techniques can reduce test anxiety and improve student self-concept, sense of locus of control, appropriate coping strategies, and test scores (Cheek, Bradley, Reynolds, & Coy, 2002; Henderson, Kelby, & Engebretson, 1992; Kiselica, Baker, Thomas, & Reedy, 1994). Thus, there is ample research to indicate that a variety of guidance curriculum interventions are excellent tools for school counseling programs.

Table 3.5. School Counseling Curriculum Interventions for Academic Achievement	
Brigman & Campbell (2003); Brigman, Webb, & Campbell (2007); Webb & Brigman (2007)	Study of impact of groups to augment the classroom curriculum materials in Student Success Skills found that there was a significant effect on academic achievement, even with students who had been considerably underachieving. This intervention has been found to be effective with students in elementary and middle school (K-9).
Carns & Carns (1991)	A curriculum intervention taught fourth-grade students about learning styles and metacognitive skills, with resultant increases in self-efficacy. Students who engaged in this intervention showed marked improvement in their academic achievement, as measured by the California Test of Basic Skills.
Gerler & Herndon (1993)	Conducted a study to evaluate the effectiveness of a 10-session, multimodal guidance unit called Succeeding in School, which was designed to improve academic performance. Students improved their awareness of how to succeed in school after the intervention, but teacher ratings of academic achievement were not significantly different from pretest to posttest.
Lee (1993)	Replicated Gerler and Herndon (1993). Teachers completed pretest and posttest ratings on students' academic achievement in math, language arts, and conduct. Found that the Succeeding in School curriculum can positively influence academic achievement in math.
Stevahn, Johnson, Johnson, & Schultz (2002)	Integrated conflict resolution materials into a high school social studies curriculum and found that students learned both the conflict resolution and the academic content more than students who didn't receive the integrated content, and were able to apply the procedures they learned more successfully.

Counseling Services

Summarizing research about counseling is challenging, as there are so many types of therapy, a wide range of client concerns, and numerous intervening variables (age, socioeconomic status, gender, presenting problem, and so on) (Kazdin & Weisz, 2003). However, meta-analytic reviews and summaries of research about counseling and therapy with children and adolescents overall find strong and consistent findings that these interventions can be quite helpful for the development of many aspects of social and emotional functioning, though they usually have only modest impacts on academic achievement (Eder & Whiston, 2006; Prout & Prout, 1998). It is useful to know that individual interventions do not have to be long-term in order to be effective, as numerous studies indicate that brief counseling can be effective in a wide variety of situations (Littrell, 1998). Counseling does seem to be a crucial component of effective comprehensive dropout prevention programs for significantly at-risk students (Edmondson & White, 1998).

What Works?

Group and individual counseling, especially when a component of a comprehensive intervention that also includes guidance lessons and/or tutoring.

The group format is a useful way to provide specific students with more information about how to be successful academically, and can also provide important opportunities for underachieving students to address emotional concerns. The research evidence suggests that small groups can positively impact academic achievement, especially when combined with interventions at the classroom or individual level. Hoag and Burlingame (1997) conducted a meta-analytic review of 49 studies about group counseling, including 9 studies that considered cognitive skills and performance, and looked at 184 outcome measures. They determined that group counseling interventions can have a moderate impact on academic achievement factors. Table 3.6 summarizes the research about group counseling.

Table 3.6. Group Interventions for School Achievement

Bailey & Bradbury-Bailey (2007)	Achievement for African American males can be effectively supported through small group work.
Brigman & Campbell (2003)	When groups are used to augment Student Success Skills classroom materials (a curriculum designed to improve academic success) with students who need that support, there can be a significant impact on academic achievement, even with students who had been considerably underachieving.
Hoag & Burlingame (1997)	Conducted a meta-analytic review of 49 studies about group counseling. Determined that group counseling interventions can have a moderate impact on academic achievement factors (Effect Size = .51).
Shechtman (2002)	Completed a review of research about child group psychotherapy. Noted that group counseling interventions for addressing school achievement need to include a social and emotional component in addition to educational remediation in order to be most effective.
Wilson (1986)	Directive counseling and behavioral counseling can have positive effects on underachieving students' academic achievement in a small group setting.

School Counseling's Indirect Impact on Student Achievement

School counselors also have indirect impact on student achievement through nonacademic interventions. Career development, social-emotional skill building, friendship groups, family meetings, stress reduction, violence prevention programs, consultation with teachers and families, college counseling, and crisis counseling are all part of the school counseling job, and most of these ways of helping students can have an impact on student achievement. Table 3.7 summarizes some of the related research. Historically, the immediate outcomes of these interventions—stress reduction, crisis resolution, social skill development—have been measured, but it is more difficult to gauge the secondary impact on academic achievement (Brown & Trusty, 2005). Minimally, however, when a child is less stressed and more successful socially, he or she is more likely to come to school, and school attendance is obviously linked to school success.

Table 3.7. School Counseling Interventions With Indirect Impact on Academic Achievement	
Bauer, Sapp, & Johnson (2000)	Cognitive-behavioral groups produced significant increases in self-esteem and academic self-concept of high school students.
Cheek, Bradley, Reynolds, & Coy (2002)	School counseling intervention helped elementary students reduce test anxiety and improve test scores.
Fouad (1995)	Found that middle school students demonstrated improved knowledge and performance in math and science courses after participating in a math and science career awareness intervention.
Grossman et al. (1997)	A study of the Second Step Violence Prevention curriculum found that observed physically aggressive behavior decreased significantly in playground and cafeteria settings and that observed neutral/prosocial behavior increased significantly in the same settings following curriculum implementation.
Henderson & Berla (1995)	Family interventions regarding social and emotional functioning can produce lower special education referrals, fewer behavioral problems, and decreases in disciplinary events.
Henderson, Kelby, & Engebretson (1992)	Classroom instruction about stress reduction techniques can help improve student self-concept, sense of locus of control, and appropriate coping strategies.
Kiselica, Baker, Thomas, & Reedy (1994)	A stress reduction program helped high school students reduce anxiety and stress-related symptoms.

In sum, the research suggests that the most efficient and effective ways for school counselors to impact student achievement are through whole-school, family-based, and/or classroom guidance interventions. Small group counseling is helpful for students who need additional support. Individual counseling interventions are helpful for a wide range of mental health concerns, but have weaker impact on academic functioning and outcomes. However, there is evidence that individual counseling can be a key component of multiapproach interventions for students who are academically at risk.

Principal-School Counselor Collaboration

The challenge of improving student achievement requires approaches that transcend old conceptions of how schools are organized and led. For instance, it has been noted that the traditional view of principals as the lone leader in schools underutilizes crucial contributions of other school staff (Lambert, 2002). The sheer complexity of improving schools requires collaborative efforts from numerous educational stakeholders (Dahir, 2000; Spillane, 2006). In response to this pressing need for collaboration to improve student achievement, the school counseling profession has increasingly emphasized the importance of collaboration—particularly with principals (ASCA, 2005; Janson, Militello, & Kosine, 2008; Stone & Dahir, 2006). Likewise, others have emphasized the importance of school counselor-principal collaboration from the perspective of the principal (Riddile & Flannery, 2008).

Impediments to Collaboration

Although principals and school counselors are uniquely situated to work collaboratively as educational leaders, a number of barriers often exist that limit such collaboration (Cobia & Henderson, 2003; House & Sears, 2002; Janson & Militello, 2007; Martin, 2002). In order for school counselors to collaborate more fully with principals in schools, their capacity to be leaders in schools needs to be emphasized (ASCA, 2005; Stone & Dahir, 2006). In contrast to principals, the idea of school counselors serving as leaders has only recently been explored in professional literature (Amatea & Clark, 2005; Shoffner & Williamson, 2000). Some possible impediments to school counselor leadership include role confusion among school counselors and principals and the resulting limitations to school counselor roles resulting from constricted relationships with principals born from this confusion.

Schools often contribute to role confusion for school counselors by defining their work as quasi-administrative (Henderson & Gysbers, 1998). Notably, there is occasionally a disconnect between the perceptions of the duties of the school counselor, with principals and schools counselors sometimes disagreeing on counseling roles and responsibilities (Amatea & Clark, 2005; Fitch, Newby, Ballestero, & Marshall, 2001; Shoffner & Williamson, 2000). Some of the tasks that principals may ask school counselors to perform, although important to the management of the school, take the school counselor away from the tasks and roles for which they were trained (Niebuhr, Niebuhr, & Cleveland, 1999). It has been noted that these tasks are often clerical and/or administrative in nature and are given to counselors by principals who are overburdened by their own work-related demands (Ribak-Rosenthal, 1994). In addition, the omission of school counselors from inclusion in decisions involving key educational issues in schools (Stone & Clark, 2001) perhaps limits school counselor collaboration with other school leaders through the assignment of tasks deemed inappropriate for school counselors.

This disagreement on counselor roles and responsibilities is further magnified by the influence principals have on shaping those roles and responsibilities (Ponec & Brock, 2000). For example, principals influence the hiring of the school counselor (Beale & McCay, 2001) and how the school counselor practices on the local level (Dahir, 2000). Consequently, unless principals are familiar with the capacity of school counselors to function as leaders, principals may not involve them in important decision-making processes that ultimately impact students and schools.

Effective Principal-School Counselor Collaboration

Despite such impediments, partnerships between principals and school counselors that focus on the shared goal of improving student achievement are occurring more frequently (Ponec & Brock, 2000; Stone & Clark, 2001). But what are the elements of effective collaboration between principals and school counselors? What are the foundations of constructive collaboration on which principals and school counselors can construct solutions within schools?

One important component of principal-school counselor collaboration is the importance of each having a firm understanding of the others' skills, capabilities, and training. It is crucial that school counselors understand the difficulty of the work of principals (Stone & Dahir, 2006). Likewise, school principals should be familiar with the emergent vision of school counseling, as proposed by the ASCA National Model (ASCA, 2005; see Appendix A). This new vision of school counseling reconfigures the role of school counselors to include a focus on systemic change, advocacy, leadership, and, yes, collaboration. Findings in one recent study suggested that, when school counselors communicate to principals the appropriate role of school counselors based on the ASCA National Model, the two share a more collaborative relationship built around leadership (Janson et al., 2008).

Another characteristic of effective partnering of principals and school counselors is a common belief in their interdependency (Janson et al., 2008; Janson & Militello, 2007; Stone & Dahir, 2006). Principals and counselors must be in agreement that they can each perform with greater effectiveness when they share support, advice, and understanding. When there is a recognition that the other adds value to not only their individual school tasks, but also to broader school leadership capacity, their effectiveness within the school is enhanced.

In many ways, familiarity with each other's roles and a shared belief in their interdependency are preconditions for collaboration. These elements compose the nature of the collaboration between principals and school counselors. However, the function of professional collaboration is critical, and it must be purposefully tied to the educational mission of schools (Spillane, 2006). For collaboration between school principals and counselors to lead to gains in student achievement and other schoolwide goals, it must be purposed for these aims. Such collaboration should focus on solutions to pressing school problems such as achievement gaps for underserved students, program development for enhancing educational opportunity, and school improvement planning (Janson et al., 2008).

Finally, it is important that structures and routines are established that facilitate purposeful collaboration between principals and school counselors (Janson, Clark, & Stone, in press). Structures and routines should either be established or reconceptualized in order to serve as vehicles for interactions that distribute leadership (Spillane, 2006). As an example, regular meetings between principals and school counselors might shift in purpose from reacting to individual student issues to including discussions as to how each will contribute to broader systemic solutions to school problems. In this way, collaboration can begin to address more complex issues that permeate today's schools.

Facilitating Collaboration in New Ways: The Distributed Leadership Model

Exhaustive lists of what one needs to do to be effective can be daunting and cause paralysis. However, if administrators and school counselors (and all other school community members) collaborate on creating effective learning communities, the work is more manageable. The growing emphasis on principal-counselor collaboration has evolved from challenges to the traditional purview of *one leader, one school*. Research has suggested that some principals and school counselors are already practicing as leaders in purposeful and collaborative ways (Janson & Militello, 2007).

One helpful framework for both understanding and structuring principal and school counselor collaborative leadership is the distributed leadership model (Janson et al., in press). Research on distributed leadership provides a modern definition of leadership that aims at shared, engaged, and meaningful work. Specifically, leadership is "the activities engaged in by leaders, in interaction with others in particular contexts around specific tasks" (Spillane, Halverson, & Diamond, 2004, p. 5). Because leadership defined this way is a construct of relationships rather than roles, a focus on what people do around activities and tasks is the appropriate unit of study (Firestone, 1996; Halverson, 2003; Spillane, 2006; Spillane et al., 2004).

Consequently, distributed leadership can lead to individual and organizational learning that can create internal reciprocal accountability (Resnick & Glennan, 2002) and comparative advantage (Elmore, 2000) in schools. Distributed leadership provides a ready-made vehicle for meaningful shared responses to reform efforts among principals and school counselors. More importantly, such leadership instills internal professionalism that may lead to changes in practice without the sanctions and mandates that often accompany reform efforts. Distributed leadership also has the capacity to innovate and support changes in practices for principals and school counselors by uncoupling these respective professionals from their traditional roles and functions, thereby allowing them to restructure their work to better meet the complex needs of schools and the students in them.

Practical Applications of Models and Research

Today's principals and school counselors are encouraged to function as change agents who create schools that support the academic achievement of all students (Paisley & Hayes, 2003). Professional standards and literature in both professions are rife with terms like collaboration, teaming, leadership, and sharing. Likewise, the relationships and interactions of school professionals have been emphasized to promote effective leadership (Crow, Hausman, & Scribner, 2002; Gronn, 2000). This chapter provided an introduction to some key ideas in both professions that might serve as a starting point for better understanding the unique challenges and rewards of both school professionals as well as the potential impact their effective partnerships might bring. While many school counselors and principals have successful working partnerships, specifics need to be identified and disseminated in order to support effective educational practices.

A useful starting place is conversation between principals and counselors, with some explicit discussion about role, function, interdependence, responsibility, and possible ways to work together toward shared outcomes. Depending on the nature of the relationships, these conversations can be formal or informal, brief or ongoing, shared with other key stakeholders, or not. However, some have suggested that more purposeful and structured interaction may provide a more conducive medium for the shared goal of improving student achievement in systematic ways (Janson & Militello, 2007, 2009).

A next step is sharing key information, particularly about the ASCA National Model (ASCA, 2005; Janson et al., 2008), relevant state models for school counseling programs (available through state departments of education), distributed leadership models (Spillane, 2006), evidence-based practice in school counseling (Dimmitt et al., 2007), data-based decision making (Holcomb, 2004; Love, 2008), and any other models or materials that might inform the structures of principal-counselor partnerships. By engaging in conversations around how school counselors can more fully join in leadership efforts to improve student achievement, principals and counselors can begin to develop shared language that allows movement toward shared practices that might improve achievement.

Once there is shared language and content knowledge, principals and school counselors can begin to identify more specific and purposeful ways of working together to achieve mutually identified key outcomes. This work has often been done rather informally. For instance, in one school, the counselor and principal go out for breakfast (early!) once a week to talk specifically about how they are supporting student learning in their school. These informal interactions are important and often occur with great intentionality, but when such interactions are planned and scheduled there is more likelihood of successful outcomes (Janson & Militello, 2009). For example, in another school, this key conversation about collaborating to support student outcomes occurs in the Student Services Team, which is facilitated by the school counselor using an agenda developed by the principal.

One important structure that can also serve as a locus for distributed leadership between principals and school counselors is a comprehensive guidance program. School counselors may move toward implementing the ASCA National Model under the guidance of their director or another administrator, or the principal may be involved directly in creating program changes. With principal support, school counselors are more able to use their unique situation in the school to use student data to make decisions about programming and scheduling, to consult with teachers and families about effective interventions for student achievement, and to make program changes that reflect what is known about effective practices and school counseling interventions. Explicit communication among counselors and principals about specific activities and programming decisions will facilitate collaboration and knowledge about outcomes.

Using evidence-based practices (Dimmitt et al., 2007), the research-based interventions and programs identified in this chapter and in the existing school counseling research summaries and meta-analyses, and institutional knowledge about what works in their specific building for their students, school counselors can have greater impact on student achievement.

School counselors and principals who have more knowledge of the models for effective practice in their respective educational domains are more likely to make effective program decisions and intervention choices. If school counselors are using interventions that have demonstrated impact on student outcomes—particularly on student achievement—then their direct contribution to the educational enterprise is clear to the principal. If the principal is practicing collaborative and distributed leadership, which allows professionals in schools to do what they do best, then school counselors can more easily be effective in their work.

What Works?
- Collaboration
- Shared language
- Understanding of roles
- Ongoing conversation
- Focus on specific outcomes
- Distributed leadership

Summary

In the midst of new accountability pressures, once again all eyes are on the school principal. Yes, real change and substantive and sustained impact on teaching and learning will require a skillful principal, but the conception of the principal as empowered by position alone must be transformed to the principal as a key leader among leaders of a professional learning community where results can be achieved and important roles are played by all. Accountability pressures, and more importantly the school reform initiatives producing these pressures, can be addressed through collaboration with skilled school counselor leaders who are implementing effective interventions and programs.

Effective leaders inspire participation, foster collaboration, and harness the strength of skills that already exist in their schools. Using such an approach, effective principals stretch leadership across key staff and around activities. They mutually engage their faculty, help colleagues share their expertise and repertoire, and view reform as a joint enterprise. School counselors can be critical partners in this effort. These key staff members, through their training, practices, and structured comprehensive counseling programs, are optimally positioned to help principals make schools more responsive and accountable to today's demands to increase achievement for all students.

Questions for Reflection

Principals and counselors, use the following questions for reflection:

1. Which of the leadership practices that contribute to academic achievement that were identified in this chapter are already occurring in your school?

2. Which of the school counseling practices that contribute to academic achievement that were identified in this chapter are already occurring in your school?

3. How do the principal and counselor(s) work together in your building? What are the shared tasks? How are roles and responsibilities decided upon? How are they communicated?

4. What would have to change in your school in order for more effective collaboration to occur between the principal and school counselor(s)?

5. What specific practices or activities would you like to implement in your school?

References

Amatea, E. S., & Clark, M. A. (2005). Changing schools, changing counselors: A qualitative study of school administrators' conceptions of the school counselor role. *Professional School Counseling, 9*(1), 16-27.

American School Counselor Association. (2005). *The ASCA National Model: A framework for school counseling programs.* Washington, DC: Author.

Bailey, D. & Bradbury-Bailey, M. (2007). Promoting achievement for African American males through group work. *Journal for Specialists in Group Work, 32*(1), 83-96.

Bauer, S. R., Sapp, M., & Johnson, D. (2000). Group counseling strategies for rural at-risk high school students. *High School Journal, 83*(2), 41-51.

Beale, A. V., & McCay, E. (2001). Selecting school counselors: What administrators should look for in prospective counselors. *The Clearing House, 74*(5), 257-260.

Borders, D. L., & Drury, S. M. (1992). Comprehensive school counseling programs: A review for policymakers and practitioners. *Journal of Counseling and Development, 70,* 487-498.

Borders, L. D., & Shoffner, M. F. (2003). School counselors: Leadership opportunities and challenges in the schools. In J. D. West, C. J. Osborn, & D. L. Bubenzer (Eds.). *Leaders and legacies: Contributions to the profession of counseling* (pp. 51-64). New York: Brunner-Routledge.

Brigman, G., & Campbell, C. (2003). Helping students improve academic achievement and school success behavior. *Professional School Counseling, 7,* 91-98.

Brigman, G., & Webb, L. (2004). *Student Success Skills: Classroom manual.* Boca Raton, FL: Atlantic Education Consultants.

Brigman, G., Webb, L., & Campbell, C. (2007). Building skills for school success: Improving the academic and social competence of students. *Professional School Counseling, 10*(3), 279-288.

Brown, D. & Trusty, J. (2005). The ASCA National Model, accountability, and establishing causal links between school counselor activities and student outcomes. *Professional School Counseling, 9*(1), 13-15.

Burns, J. M. (1978). *Leadership*. New York: Harper & Row.

Carns, A. W., & Carns, M. R. (1991). Teaching study skills, cognitive strategies, and metacognitive skills through self-diagnosed learning styles. *ASCA School Counselor, 38*, 341-346.

Carty, L., Rosenbaum, J. N., Lafreniere, K., & Sutton, J. (2000). Peer group counseling: An intervention that works. *Guidance and Counseling, 15*(2), 2-8.

Casey, R. J., & Berman, J. S. (1985). The outcome of psychotherapy with children. *Psychological Bulletin, 98*, 388-400.

Cheek, J. R., Bradley, L. J., Reynolds, J., & Coy, D. (2002). An intervention for helping elementary students reduce test anxiety. *Professional School Counseling, 6*(2), 162-165.

Clark, M. A., & Stone, C. B. (2000). Evolving our image: School counselors as educational leaders. *Counseling Today, 42*(11), 21-22, 29, 46.

Cobia, D., & Henderson, D. (2003). *Handbook of school counseling*. Columbus, OH: Merrill-Prentice Hall.

Crow, G., Hausman, C. S., & Scribner, J. P. (2002). Reshaping the principalship. In J. Murphy (Ed.), *The educational leadership challenge* (pp. 189-210). Chicago: University of Chicago Press.

Dahir, C. A. (2000). Principals as partners in school counseling. *The ASCA Counselor, 38*(2), 13.

Darling-Hammond, L., LaPointe, M., Meyerson, D., & Orr, M. (2007). *Preparing school leaders for a changing world: Lessons from exemplary leadership development programs*. Stanford, CA: Stanford University, Stanford Educational Leadership Institute.

Deal, T. E., & Peterson, K. (1998). *Shaping school culture: The heart of leadership*. San Francisco: Jossey-Bass.

Dimmitt, C., Carey, J. C., & Hatch, T. (2007). *Evidence-based school counseling: Making a difference with data-driven practice*. Thousand Oaks, CA: Corwin Press.

Eder, K., & Whiston, S. (2006). Does psychotherapy help some students? An overview of psychotherapy outcome research. *Professional School Counseling, 9*(5), 337-343.

Edmondson, J. H., & White, J. (1998). A tutorial and counseling program: Helping students at risk of dropping out of school. *Professional School Counseling, 1*(4), 43-51.

Elmore, R. (2000). *Building a new structure for school leadership.* Washington, DC: Albert Shanker Institute.

Elmore, R. (2003). Accountability and capacity. In M. Carnoy, R. Elmore & L. S. Siskin (Eds.), *The new accountability: High schools and high-stakes testing* (pp. 195-209). New York: RoutledgeFalmer.

Elmore, R. (2004). The problem of stakes in performance-based accountability systems. In S. H. Fuhrman & R. Elmore (Eds.), *Redesigning accountability systems for education* (pp. 274-296). New York: Teachers College Press.

Embry, D. D., Flannery, D. J., Vazsonyi, T. T., Powell, K. E., & Atha, H. (1996). PeaceBuilders: A theoretically driven, school-based model for early violence prevention. *American Journal of Preventive Medicine, 12*(5 supplement), 91-100.

Firestone, W. (1996). Leadership roles or functions? In K. Leithwood, D. Chapman, P. Corson, P. Hallinger, & A. Hart (Eds.), *International handbook of educational leadership and administration* (pp. 395-418). Boston: Kluwer Academic Publishers.

Fitch, T., Newby, E., Ballestero, V., & Marshall, J. L. (2001). Future school administrators' perceptions of the school counselor's role. *Counselor Education and Supervision, 41*, 89-99.

Flannery, D. J., Vazsonyi, A. T., Liau, A. K., Guo, S., Powell, K. E., Atha, H., et al. (2003). Initial behavior outcomes for the Peacebuilders universal school-based violence prevention program. *Developmental Psychology, 39*(2), 292-308.

Fouad, N. A. (1995). Career linking: An intervention to promote math and science career awareness. *Journal of Counseling & Development, 73*, 527-534.

Gerler, E. R., Jr. (1985). Elementary school counseling research and the classroom learning environment. *Elementary School Guidance and Counseling, 20*, 39-48.

Gerler, E. R., & Herndon, E. Y. (1993). Learning how to succeed academically in middle school. *Elementary School Guidance and Counseling, 27*(3), 186-197.

Gronn, P. (2000). Distributed properties: A new architecture for leadership. *Educational Management and Administration, 28*(3), 317-338.

Grossman, D. C., Neckerman, H. J., Koepsell, T. D., Liu, P., Asher, K. N., Beland, K., et al. (1997). Effectiveness of a violence prevention curriculum among children in elementary school. *Journal of the American Medical Association, 227*(20), 1605-1611.

Hallinger, P., & Heck, R. (1996). Reassessing the principal's role in school effectiveness: A review of empirical research, 1980-1995. *Education Administration Quarterly, 32*(1), 5-44.

Halverson, R. (2003). Systems of practice: How leaders use artifacts to create professional community in schools. *Educational Policy Analysis Archives, 11*(37), 1-35.

Heifetz, R. A., & Linsky, M. (2002). *Leadership on the line: Staying alive through the dangers of leading.* Boston: Harvard Business School Press.

Henderson, A. T., & Berla, N. (1995). *A new generation of evidence: The family is critical to student achievement.* Washington, DC: Center for Law and Education.

Henderson, P., & Gysbers, N. C. (1998). *Leading and managing your school guidance staff: A manual for school administrators and directors of guidance.* Alexandria, VA: American Counseling Association.

Henderson, P. A., Kelby, T. J., & Engebretson, K. M. (1992). Effects of a stress-control program on children's locus of control, self-concept, and coping behavior. *The School Counselor, 40*, 125-130.

Hoag, M. J., & Burlingame, G. M. (1997). Evaluating the effectiveness of child and adolescent group treatment: A meta-analytic review. *Journal of Clinical Child Psychology, 26*(3), 234-246.

Holcomb, E. L. (2004). *Getting excited about data* (2nd ed.). Thousand Oaks, CA: Corwin Press.

House, R. M., & Hayes, R. L. (2002). School counselors: Becoming key players in school reform. *Professional School Counseling, 5*(4), 249-256.

House, R. M., & Martin, P. J. (1998). Advocating for better futures for all students: A new vision for school counselors. *Education, 119*, 284-291.

House, R., & Sears, S. (2002). Preparing school counselors to be leaders and advocates: A critical need in the new millennium. *Theory Into Practice, 41*(3), 154-162.

Janson, C., Clark, M. A., & Stone, C. (in press). Stretching leadership: A distributed perspective for school counselor leaders. *Professional School Counseling.*

Janson, C. & Militello, M. (2007, March). *Enhancing the relationship of school principals and counselors.* Paper presented at the 2007 Annual Convention of the American Counseling Association, Detroit, MI.

Janson, C. & Militello, M. (2009, April). *Are we there yet? Factors that foster and inhibit urban school counseling reform.* Paper presented at the annual meeting of the American Educational Research Association, San Diego, CA.

Janson, C., Militello, M., & Kosine, N. (2008). Four views of the professional school counselor-principal relationship: A Q methodology study. *Professional School Counseling, 11*(6), 353-361.

Kazdin, A. E., & Weisz, J. R. (Eds.). (2003). *Evidence-based psychotherapies for children and adolescents.* New York: Guilford Press.

Kern, C. W. (1999). Professional school counselors: Inservice providers who can change the school environment. *NASSP Bulletin, 83*(603), 10-17.

Kiselica, M. S., Baker, S. B., Thomas, R. N. & Reedy, S. (1994). Effects of stress inoculation training on anxiety, stress, and academic performance of adolescents. *Journal of Counseling Psychology, 41*, 335-342.

Lambert, L. (2002). A framework for shared leadership. *Educational Leadership, 59*(8), 37-40.

Lapan, R. T., Gysbers, N. C., & Petroski, G. F. (2001). Helping seventh graders be safe and successful: A statewide study of the impact of comprehensive guidance and counseling programs. *Journal of Counseling & Development, 79*, 320-330.

Lapan, R. T., Gysbers, N. C., & Sun, Y. (1997). The impact of more fully implemented guidance programs on the school experiences of high school students: A statewide evaluation study. *Journal of Counseling & Development, 75*, 292-302.

Lee, R. S. (1993). Effects of classroom guidance on student achievement. *Elementary School Guidance and Counseling, 27,* 163-171.

Leithwood, K., Seashore Louis, K., Anderson, S., & Wahlstrom, K. (2004). *How leadership influences student learning.* New York: Wallace Foundation.

Littrell, J. M. (1998). *Brief counseling in action.* New York: Norton.

Love, N. (2008). *Using data to improve learning for all: A collaborative inquiry approach.* Thousand Oaks, CA: Corwin Press.

Luiselli, J. K., Putnam, R. F., Handler, M. W., & Feinberg, A. B. (2005). Whole-school positive behavior support: Effects on student discipline problems and academic performance. *Educational Psychology, 25*(2/3), 183–198.

Marks, H. M., & Printy, S. M. (2003). Principal leadership and school performance: An integration of transformations and instructional leadership. *Educational Administration Quarterly, 39*(3), 370-397.

Martin, P. (2002). Transforming school counseling: A national perspective. *Theory into Practice, 41*(3), 148-153.

Marzano, R. J., Waters, T., & McNulty, B. (2005). *School leadership that works: From research to results.* Alexandria, VA: Association for Supervision and Curriculum Development.

McGannon, W., Carey, J. C., & Dimmitt, C. (2006). The current status of school counseling outcome research. *What Works in School Counseling, 1,* 14-29.

Millitello, M., Rallis, S., & Goldring, E. (2009). *Leading with inquiry and action: How principals improve teaching and learning.* Thousand Oaks, CA: Corwin Press.

Moore-Johnson, S. (1996). *Leading to change: The challenge of the new superintendency.* San Francisco: Jossey-Bass.

Nelson, J. R., Martella, R. M., & Marchand-Martella, N. (2002). Maximizing student learning: The effects of a comprehensive school-based program for preventing problem behaviors. *Journal of Emotional and Behavioral Disorders, 10*(3), 136-148.

Newman-Carlson, D., & Horne, A. M. (2004). BullyBusters: A psychoeducational intervention for reducing bullying behaviors in middle school students. *Journal of Counseling and Development, 82,* 259-267.

Newman, F., King, B., & Young, P. (2000). *Professional development that addresses school capacity: Lessons from urban elementary schools.* Paper presented at the annual meeting of the American Educational Research Association, New Orleans, LA.

Niebuhr, K. E., Niebuhr, R. E., & Cleveland, W. T. (1999). Principal and counselor collaboration. *Education, 119,* 674-678.

Paisley, P. O., & Hayes, R. L. (2003). School counseling in the academic domain: Transformations in preparation and practice. *Professional School Counseling, 6*(3), 198-204.

Ponec, D. L., & Brock, B. L. (2000). Relationships among elementary school counselors and principals: A unique bond. *Professional School Counseling, 3,* 208-217.

Printy, S. M. (2008). Leadership for teacher learning: A community of practice perspective. *Educational Administration Quarterly, 44*(2), 187-226.

Prout, H. T., & DeMartino, R. A. (1986). A meta-analysis of school-based decision making for school counseling. *Professional School Counseling, 10,* 121-130.

Prout, S. M., & Prout, H. T. (1998). A meta-analysis of school-based studies of counseling and psychotherapy: An update. *Journal of School Psychology, 36,* 121-136

Resnick, L. B., & Glennan, T. K. (2002). Leadership for learning: A theory of action for urban school districts. In A. Hightower, M. S. Knapp, J. A. Marsh & M. W. McLaughlin (Eds.), *Schools districts and instructional renewal* (pp. 160-172). New York: Teachers College Press.

Ribak-Rosenthal, N. (1994). Reasons individuals become school administrators, school counselors, and teachers. *The School Counselor, 41,* 158-164.

Riddile, M., & Flanary, R. A. (2008, August/September). Principal and counselor collaboration. *College Board Connection.* Retrieved September 24, 2008, from http://www.connection-collegeboard.com/08sep/commentary.html

Schectman, Z. (1993). Child group psychotherapy in the school at the threshold of a new millennium. *Journal of Counseling and Development, 80,* 257-384.

Schlossberg, S. M., Morris, J. D., & Lieberman, M. G. (2001). The effects of a counselor-led guidance intervention on students' behaviors and attitudes. *Professional School Counseling, 4,* 156-164.

Shoffner, M. F., & Williamson, R. D. (2000). Engaging preservice school counselors and principals in dialogue and collaboration. *Counselor Education and Supervision, 40*(2), 128-141.

Sink, C. A., & Stroh, H. R. (2003). Raising achievement test scores of early elementary school students through comprehensive school counseling programs. *Professional School Counseling, 6*(5), 350-365.

Spillane, J. (2006). *Distributed leadership*. San Francisco: Jossey-Bass.

Spillane, J., Halverson, R., & Diamond, J. B. (2004). Toward a theory of leadership practice: A distributed perspective. *Journal of Curriculum Studies, 36*(1), 3-34.

Stevahn, L., Johnson, D. W., Johnson, R. T., & Schultz, R. (2002). Effects of conflict resolution training integrated into a high school social studies curriculum. *Journal of Social Psychology, 142*(3), 305-331.

Stone, C., & Clark, M. A. (2001). School counselors and principals: Partners in support of academic achievement. *National Association of Secondary School Principals Bulletin, 85*(624), 46-53.

Stone, C., & Dahir, C. (2006). *The transformed school counselor*. Boston: Houghton Mifflin.

United States Department of Education. (2009). *What Works Clearinghouse.* Retrieved June 28, 2009, from http://ies.ed.gov/ncee/wwc/

Vazsonyi, A. T., Bellison, L. M., & Flannery, D. J. (2004). Evaluation of a school-based, universal violence prevention program: Low-, medium-, and high risk children. *Youth Violence and Juvenile Justice, 2*(2), 185-206.

Webb, L., & Brigman, G. (2007). Student success skills: A structured group intervention for school counselors. *Journal for Specialists in Group Work, 32*(2), 190-201.

Wenger, E. (1999). *Communities of practice: Learning, meaning and identity*. New York: Cambridge University Press.

Whiston, S. C., & Sexton, T. L. (1998). A review of school counseling outcome research: Implications for practice. *Journal of Counseling & Development, 76*, 412-426.

Wilson, N. S. (1986). Counselor interventions with low-achieving and underachieving elementary, middle, and high school students: A review of the literature. *Journal of Counseling & Development, 64*, 628-634.

Chapter 4
Beyond Serendipity: Intentional Principal and School Counselor Collaboration and Inquiry

Chris Janson and Matthew Militello

Our Challenge

In this chapter we investigate how specific roles in schools are fostering the process of change and school improvement. We focus on the principal and counselor as actors in a school working through collaborative change. This chapter is informed by our own experiences working side-by-side as a high school counselor and assistant principal, as well as our collaboration on research focused on distributed leadership practices of school principals and counselors.

Distributed leadership allows the expertise of individuals to be brought to bear around specific problems. This shift allows roles to change and provides multiple experts in schools.

Chris Janson, Ph.D., is an Assistant Professor in the Department of Leadership, Counseling and Instructional Technology at the University of North Florida. Email c.janson@unf.edu. Matthew Militello, Ph.D., is an Assistant Professor of Educational Leadership and Policy Studies at North Carolina State University. Email matt_militello@ncsu.edu. Janson and Militello previously worked together in the same high school in Michigan, where Janson was a school counselor and Militello was an assistant principal.

The *function* of education has remained static throughout history. That is, across cultures and time, education continues to be viewed as the tonic for what ails society. However, schooling, the process of education, has taken on many *forms*. Nonetheless, the form of schooling in the United States has remained generally static. Specifically, the rigidness of the classroom structures and the units of study (school schedule and content) have created specialization among actors in schools. Teachers teach, principals lead, and counselors counsel.

Overspecialization makes change difficult. Change theory provides a tenuous juxtaposition to the static organization. Change involves problem identification, acceptance, collaborative action, and evaluation and reflection.

There are pitfalls in every step: Is the identified problem *focused on* or *distracting from* student learning (Identify Problem)? How do we get different people with often competing agendas to agree on the problem (Acceptance)? Are people willing and able to engage in new practices (Collaborative Action)? And, how do we dialogue and analyze data to understand the impact of change (Evaluation and Reflection)? While the change process is highly personal, *real* change—that has both staying power and power to impact outcomes (e.g., student learning)—requires sharing what we know and engaging in what we do to achieve agreed-upon ends.

In short, there are no shortcuts for change—the work is difficult. The justification for the calls for change and a new order of practices in our schools lies in the core product of K-12 education: the cognitive and affective growth of students to be learned in content and informed of their rights and responsibilities as citizens. This will require school actors to perform collaboratively and righteously.

Our Story

We chose to use a play script as our medium rather than following a pattern of either a step-by-step prescription of what needs to be done or a highly academic account that only provides an amalgamation of theories.[1] We found our balance of theory and practice in a play's dialogic format. Our play is typical in that it follows the traditional format of three acts. Rather than introduce an antagonist as one person, the school organization as the antagonist represents traditions of schooling (e.g., finance, time, relationship). Our aim is to provide a story that provides insights and strategies for change in schools. Additionally, we seek to uncover the power and importance of the vital relationship between counselors and principals to make this happen.

Act One: The Problem
Scene 1: High School Cafeteria

Two simultaneous reflections are occurring. In the first, Chris, a school counselor, is reflecting on a conversation he had with a student while eating in the school cafeteria. In the second conversation, Matt, the school principal, is muttering to himself as he walks through the cafeteria on his way back to his office.

CHRIS

I can't help but wonder what's going on behind the scenes here. This is the third time Manuel has come to see me in the past 2 weeks wanting to have conversations about whether he is a "good fit" at the high school. That maybe the alternative school is better for him.

---

1 Portions of this dramatization are taken from a classroom teaching exercise (Janson, 2008; Militello, 2007).

It's a little unsettling to me how a couple of staff members have not only planted this seed, but are now bent on nurturing its growth until Manuel is placed out of the school here. I think Manuel is confused, and I can see why. He isn't happy here, that's certain. But is he now looking to take advantage of this "invitation" from two of his teachers—two teachers he readily admits he could do without? I'm not sure at all that moving buildings is better for Manuel. What disturbs me most is that I know teachers and other staff have had similar conversations with Manuel's sister and one of his best friends. How long before they're sitting with me and I'm having the same conversations? It feels like I can predict right now who will be pushed or self-select into the alternative program. It just doesn't feel right.

Matt

I spend all day escorting students to and from that art class. Ever since we created the stipulation that office referral would be attached to our alternative school selection process, Ellis has been constantly sending certain kids out of class. Now he is mad when I immediately walk a student back to class and inform him that the "infraction" is not a referral and should be handled in class. But I am afraid it is too late. I feel that Ellis is targeting students that he no longer wants in his class. Now the simplest of instructions has become a battle between teacher and student. Of course, this is not all the teacher's fault, but now that he "has it out" for these students, they push his buttons to elicit a response. I think Ellis has put me in a similar position. I find myself marching kids back into the classroom and providing prosecutor-like details on the inappropriateness of his actions. I am counseling both the teacher and the students. And I am having more rational conversations with the students! I think what disturbs me the most is the "type" of student that I most typically see in my office—and not only from Ellis. At a recent staff meeting I discussed the importance and difficulties with "managing heterogeneity." Our student body is heterogeneous in many ways—ethnically, religiously, linguistically, culturally, and in regard to their interests. However, I am beginning to see a pattern of referral that leads me to believe that some of our celebrated heterogeneity may be in jeopardy. Specifically, the students that do not "look like" or "act like" the traditional image of a high school student that our staff may have are being encouraged to look elsewhere. What happens if we begin to send a certain group of students to the alternative school? What happens if a certain group becomes disenfranchised and chooses to drop out of school? What happens if we lose our heterogeneity? Do we want homogenous groups in our high school, alternative school, and on the street? It just doesn't feel right.

Although the initial focus was on examining and altering the student referral process for alternative placement, deeper, underlying issues and assumptions about current practice were uncovered.

Scene 2: High School Conference Room

A monthly alternative placement meeting assembles to discuss who should be transitioned to the alternative high school. The standing group includes: Cheri (principal at the alternative high school), Mary Beth (the school social worker), Ellis (high school art teacher), Liz (high school math teacher), Matt (high school principal), and Chris (high school counselor).

CHERI

Okay, folks. We meet again. Just to let you know we have five open spots at the moment. As always, let's discuss the students you have the most concerns about first.

MARY BETH

I'll start then. I really have deep concerns about a handful of students, but I'll start with Manuel. He's really been floundering here for a long time. He just can't seem to pull it together. I think that an alternative setting will give him a lot more room to move. He's not the kind of student that can sit through a normal school day. It's too rigid for him. Plus, I talked to him and he wants to go. His best friend has been there since last semester so that will ease the transition.

ELLIS

I couldn't agree more about the need for Manuel to go. I think it'd be better for him and better for the rest of the students here. Some of these kids are so hardcore. It's almost impossible to reach them, and, when I try to, the whole flow of the class is disrupted. Then I'm not meeting anybody's needs.

LIZ

I just want to make sure that we're really making decisions about these kids with their best interests in mind. Have we tried everything that we can here before sending them on? I mean, I feel that there's got to be something more I could be doing somehow. You say Manuel needs "movement." Does that mean he is a kinesthetic learner? And, if so, have we tried teaching him in that fashion? I'm very uneasy about this. Are we making these transitions for the kids or for us?

Ellis

What do you mean? We already bend over backwards and try every strategy—how much time can you spend on one or two kids? It doesn't get more kinesthetic and hands-on in art. Liz—come on, we shouldn't be working harder than they are. Maybe they just need a fresh start.

Liz

I don't know; I hear what you're saying, but I also know some teachers in school—including me—don't know or haven't tried everything we can. I can't quite put my finger on it. You know, what makes the alternative school a better fit? What do they teach there? I met the math teacher once to give him books that we haven't used in years, and he was so grateful. Is that a sign of what students are moving to?

Cheri

I'll tell you one thing. We do the absolute best we can for kids. We try to get a picture of the complete child. Do teachers here know about the kids' home lives? I know ours do. Don't get me wrong—we have our struggles—but Liz is right. We get the district's leftovers all the way around—books, teachers, and students. We have no custodians; our teachers clean their own rooms. But we make do to try to do right by kids.

Chris

Cheri, no one is questioning your commitment. I think Liz is spot on. We need to focus on what is the best educational decision for Manuel and the other students on your lists.

Mary Beth

That's what we're trying to do. These students on my list, especially Manuel, want this. In his case, I've spent a lot of time explaining his options to his mom. She wants this, too. Why are we holding him back here? Bottom line, it doesn't matter how new and fresh his books are, or his teachers, if he's just going to get himself expelled.

Matt

Perhaps, but I have the feeling that this conversation is no longer about Manuel. Manuel simply represents a larger issue.

Ellis

We can have such philosophical conversations later, but it seems to me there is room at the alternative setting and consensus from Manuel's teachers and caseworker. Can we move on to the next one? I would like to discuss …

Matt

(Glancing across the table to Chris and addressing him directly) Let's make sure we get together at some point after this meeting is over. There are a few things I want to catch you up on.

Individually, principals and counselors have vital positions at two fulcrums of student data. However, by pooling the capacity for data use inherent in each position, the potential for using data to drive school reform is exponentially expanded.

Scene 3: Local Establishment

Matt and Chris meet after school to debrief on the placement meeting.

<u>CHRIS</u>

I can't stop thinking about the meeting this morning.

<u>MATT</u>

I know it. People were saying a lot in codes. What does "needs room" or "hardcore" or "better for him and the rest of the class" mean? To me it was simply code for "get this kid out of my class!"

<u>CHRIS</u>

I felt that too. Aside from the positions about individual students, it's so disturbing that the bulk of those referrals are male Latino students. What does that say?

<u>MATT</u>

That's right. Was that conversation about students or teachers? It's hard not to think that some of that was about making teaching easier by removing challenging students. It's cloaked in talk about the interests of the students, though. It is also interesting that this committee has never included teachers from the alternative school. I think a major consequence of this is that they have no voice in who attends their school, they do not have a venue to provide guidance to working with students with different needs in the regular high school setting, and, most disturbing, they are unable to support the transition of students back to the high school. Have we set this system up to track one type of student into the alternative school, isolated and marginalized the alternative school teachers, and given students a life sentence in the alternative school?

Chris

I don't like a lot of what Ellis said, but ultimately he's right. Those students are not getting their needs met. We don't have supports in place—for students or teachers. It makes it tricky to confront staff members around these placement decisions.

Matt

Whatever we do, we have to stem the tide of leakage of certain students into the alternative school. And we need to find out what needs to be done at our high school to better serve our population.

Chris

Absolutely. It's so disproportionate. Listen to this data I tracked down. These are the referral lists from the last year. I have also included a list of current enrollment over there. There are some pretty ominous trends from the standpoint of ethnicity.

Matt

That's interesting that you brought up data. I was looking at data regarding the staffing at the alternative school. What we know is that the most challenged kids in terms of learning need the best teachers. Look at this, though. Big surprise! The alternative school doesn't have any highly qualified teachers. Their enrollment has a high ratio of students receiving special education services, yet they have the least-experienced teachers with the least training. I don't know how Cheri does it. She's going to burn out. She's going to leave.

CHRIS

We've got to do something. It's a huge relief that it did not feel right to you either. Aren't we just sending our more challenged—and challenging—students to an environment that has far fewer resources? I sat in that meeting feeling such a sense of inertia. Things just start rolling toward these decisions that will have huge ramifications for the students. Cheri is key to how we can better think about this. She knows her school and the kids that we're sending over there so well.

MATT

We also need to share the data we've found. We have to focus on the numbers. I mean, what other data do we have or need and what would it say? We need to give the others a chance to come to these conclusions by looking at these and other data. That is, we cannot move to solutions to rectify the problem without everyone being on board. We must have individual acceptance that the problem is real and that it is the team's responsibility to work on it.

CHRIS

I know I sound like an administrator, but we should convene another committee to look into this. We have a clear problem of practice. Let's get folks together to play with all the data we have on students—achievement, discipline, and student climate data—and on our programs. Let's get acceptance with the facts and a reminder of our profession—to help ALL students advance their knowledge and skills.

Distributed leadership "presses us to consider organizational structure as more than a vessel for leadership activity" by emphasizing the interplay between these structures and the leaders who work within them (Spillane, Halverson, & Diamond, 2001, p. 26).

Act II: Seeking Acceptance
Scene 1: High School Conference Room

Matt and Chris convene a meeting to review the data they collected together. The participants include the entire alternative placement committee along with a few new members: Danita (district assistant superintendent for curriculum and instruction), Mark (high school special education teacher), and Eva and Bailey (teachers at the alternative high school).

MATT

First, I want to thank you all for coming to this meeting on such short notice. I know either Chris or I spoke with each of you as we scheduled this, but I want to quickly frame some of the issues we're here to talk about today. Following our last alternative placement meeting, Chris and I got together with Cheri with the intention of more closely examining the district's alternative placement process and also looking at some of the data relating to the alternative high school. That conversation led us to start thinking about some of the larger issues for both of the high schools. I have invited Danita to join us so that the central office is well informed and can provide additional insight into our work.

CHERI

I shared with Matt and Chris our most recent student performance data at the alternative high school. Although, for the most part, students have earned better grades after transferring to us, there is a need to better understand why that is taking place. It could be a lot of things—some good, some bad. Over here, we'd like to think that the change lets kids rethink their purpose. We'd also like to think that the change in learning environment is more conducive to better academic performance, that they find a "safe" place for their learning. Those are the good things. However, we have also taken this as an opportunity to start thinking about the curricula that we have in place. Are they anchored properly in standards? Are our teachers fully equipped to meet the needs of our students—both in their content knowledge and their teaching skills? Is the grading employed at our school as rigorous as what the students experienced before? Questions like this have been often uttered, but little has been done to find out the answers.

CHRIS

That's right Cheri. It is important that we talk not only about how and why we're selecting students for alternative placement, but also the nature of their learning experiences before and after any transition. This grew out of questions surrounding why we are seeing students from similar groups overpopulating our referral meetings. How are we not meeting the needs of those students here? Are we always really helping them by sending them on to the alternative school?

MARY BETH

I think we need to focus on what is manageable at this point. Cheri said herself that the students are doing better at her school. They're happier, too, and the two are certainly related. Why now do we have to put the alternative high school on the spot and make them prove themselves to us? They have already proven themselves to the kids that are there.

CHERI

No, no. I don't feel that this is about us being on the spot here. This is about figuring out what's best for kids. We can no longer rely on "moving kids from one school to another" as meaningful data to answer the question about "what's best for kids?"

MATT

Mary Beth, what we're saying is that the main focus of today is to look beyond our existing process for how we're making decisions about kids. The more Cheri, Chris, and I have talked since our last meeting, the more we're seeing how connected many of these issues are. We've always had a referral process to the alternative school, but have we examined what we can do here for some of those kids first? Are we referring kids for the right reasons? And once we refer them, are we providing Cheri and her staff with the support they need for kids that were difficult for some of us here? And, is there a process in place to transfer students back to our high school?

MARY BETH

Well, all those issues are interesting and worth exploring. But is that what we are here for? I thought this was about kids and putting them in places that best serve their needs.

DANITA

But what do you know about the kids you are referring out? Besides referral data, what do you know about the kids—their learning, their homes, their needs?

CHRIS

We don't have all that data yet. Moreover, what we do have is disturbing. Take a look at this chart [passing around a data report on enrollment trends at the alternative school over the past 3 years].

LIZ

Wow! This is an eye-opener. Have we really been sending this many students of color over there? It's powerful to see this data broken down.

DANITA

It is a concern, without a doubt. We need to gain some kind of understanding about what these numbers mean. Clearly, though, there's a problem. It's not like our district is very diverse to begin with. As I see it, this raises questions about why we refer kids. Like I said before, what do we know about these kids other than teachers think they do not "fit" at the traditional school? Should we only use referral as the variable to admissions and grades as the metric for success? Seems that these are issues that have led you all to this point.

MARK

So what we know and don't know needs to be addressed. We also should be talking about how to measure success at the alternative school.

DANITA

Not only how to measure success, but how to ensure success.

ELLIS

I just don't think we can be all things to all kids. The alternative school is there for a reason. To provide a better fit in terms of learning environment for students who, for whatever reasons, weren't prospering here. They go there and they generally graduate—or at least are more likely to do so than they would be here. Cheri and her staff should be applauded.

BAILEY

Thanks Ellis, but Danita raises an interesting point. There's no doubt that we work hard to help all students get through to graduation. For some kids, their placements make so much sense. They seem to need the smaller, personalized environment we have over there. To be honest, though, with others I'm not so sure. And again, we will work hard for all kids, but it just seems that some students find their way to us not because our environment is more conducive, but because they seem to be escaping from or squeezed out of your school. If students end up here only because of learning style mismatches, I think that's a problem. Therefore, we need to know more about our students, but also more about us as teachers. What do we do well? What do we need to do better?

LIZ

I think we have to ask some tough questions. If it's not about grades, then what is it all about? Why are so many of our struggling students from diverse backgrounds? Do we as a staff, as a district, know how to best reach these kids? And what is different about the alternative setting for them? Can we learn from what they're doing and apply that here?

Matt

Those are exactly some of the questions we need to address. We need to combine multiple sources of data to develop a more complete understanding of what is needed. Only then can we move to identify possible solutions that benefit students and teachers at both schools. For instance, Liz said at the last meeting that she thought the math classes at the alternative school were using old books, and she wondered what kind of curricular support they had. Well, Cheri looked into that and it is true about them using a hodgepodge of our discarded textbooks. More troubling is that they are indeed mostly going it alone over there without curricular support from our teachers or any other district representative. With a more complete understanding of the problem, we can develop more effective and efficient solutions.

Liz

I've been thinking about some things that I can do. For one, I'd like to start meeting with the math teachers at your school, Cheri. Seeing if together we can start filling any gaps that might exist between our math curricula. That's a start. I also think that our math teachers could learn from your teachers about how to build rapport with their students. I mean, that's one of the main reasons kids cite for leaving, isn't it? That no one cares about them here. We need to think about mentoring students as individuals, not just shepherding their learning in math.

Eva

I don't think I speak just for myself when I say that we would welcome more ongoing conversations with you and other teachers in the district, Liz. I think it could help students and staff.

DANITA

That could be a strong model for all departments, Liz. It wouldn't hurt to build more cohesion between all content areas.

CHRIS

Teaching assignments for our district staff are something else that we've been examining. We feel that thinking about teaching assignments differently holds some possibilities for addressing some of the issues, too.

MATT

That's right, Chris. We looked up data on highly qualified teacher status. I don't think it's a shock to anyone that our most experienced teachers, usually our best teachers, are the ones who are teaching most of the honors and AP courses at our traditional high school.

CHRIS

What would happen if some of our best teachers were not solely focused on our high-achieving students?

MARK

Let's wait a minute. What should we do? Tell teachers what classes they'll be teaching? Don't teachers earn the right through their years of service to teach what feeds their souls? I'm not sure we can help students by punishing teachers. That's probably even a union issue. Not to mention the number of parents that will be at your door, Matt, if they think you want to take the best teachers away from their children.

Danita

Let's be clear. We need to make decisions around what's best for students, not what's best for staff. It's not easy, though. There are staff morale issues to deal with, but we need to address those separately. Matt, Chris, what are you thinking about in terms of teaching assignments?

Chris

One thing we've talked about with Cheri is how powerful it would be having some of our advanced placement teachers teaching at her school, too. Maybe they could even co-teach with the staff there. That way there would be some modeling and mentoring as well.

Matt

I know I could mandate this as the building principal, but that would only cause animosity. I would like for us as a group to make the case for this using the data we have and identifying additional data we need. We should create a unified front that includes some possible solutions. However, I do believe that our teachers will come up with some solutions of their own that will be effective.

Chris

Yes. I was talking to our counseling staff about this just yesterday and they are beginning to look at what they can do about this situation. We also began to discuss the students we have sent to the alternative school. What have we been doing to support their career and college aspirations? The answer alarmed us. We realized that we need to be an integral part of the development of students in both schools.

C<small>HERI</small>

I feel relieved about where this conversation has gone today. I know this is just a first little step. Thinking about how we're doing things now and how we can do things differently is a great first step.

M<small>ATT</small>

The challenge now is to alter our practices. We need to think about how we share ownership of some of these ideas so they're doable and manageable. That's the hard work, because we know there'll be resistance to a lot of these ideas. Even if everyone here is on board, we have two school staffs to work with, to convince. Let me suggest that we spend the rest of our time today fleshing out some of the ideas expressed here so we can begin moving forward on some of them.

What fosters or inhibits change? How have the content (what) and context (how) changed? Is the school staff building motivation to make necessary changes? Is the staff increasing capacity (knowledge and ability to make necessary changes)? Are the changes systemic? Are the changes sustainable? What is the ultimate impact on student achievement?

Act III: Moving Toward New Practice
Scene I: District Office Meeting Room Months Later

Danita meets with Matt and Chris to discuss progress resulting from initiatives that grew from the previous semester's meetings with district leaders.

MATT

Hi, Danita. I wanted to give you a copy of this binder we are now using for admissions for the alternative school. I also included the summaries of our school climate and learning surveys that the counseling office administered to students at both schools. I have been using these data at our schoolwide meetings. Teachers have been appalled by some of the data. For instance, they were disturbed that so many students did not feel they had a strong adult relationship in the building, and that a majority of students did not feel that they were taught in ways that matched their learning style.

CHRIS

It was amazing to watch the staff come up with solutions and think about teaching practices in the classroom.

DANITA

What types of solutions, Chris?

Chris

For instance, the counseling office is working closely with teachers at both schools to make sure every student has a mentor who knows him or her personally. And a number of the mentors and mentees are between the two high schools!

Matt

Chris is being modest. That is only one solution that has been generated. Chris and the counselors have been providing career and academic guidance lessons at the alternative school.

Chris

And they're going well. I meet with Cheri and her staff each Tuesday when we process the activities from the previous week and continue to develop others. They've really embraced it, and many of the students there seem to appreciate them. I helped deliver one last week on financial aid and saw Liz there with Eva and another one of their math teachers.

Danita

Great! I talked with Cheri earlier today, and she said that she thought the teachers there appreciated being able to have discrete time to deal with career and academic concerns. She said that they always felt the need for this, but were unsure of how to squeeze it into their days. Now they are better able to have those conversations because there is time allocated for it. You said you saw Liz. Is she going over there regularly, Matt?

How might the changes and interventions that grew from them be nurtured into sustainable, systemic changes?

MATT

Yes. She's been meeting with them pretty regularly. I think it's had an impact on their curriculum. At least they're working with the same math curriculum in both schools now. However, we have not been as successful with getting our advanced placement teachers over there. I have spoken to two of our best AP teachers, Dylan and Dominic, but there is some resistance to spending part of the day at the alternative school.

DANITA

You can't change everything and everybody right away. Focus on what is working and find ways to support, sustain, and publicize the good work. Success breeds success.

CHRIS

Danita, we have also been in discussion with the Latino Cultural Center in town about mentoring students in the two high schools. On top of that, they are willing to work with our staff to provide professional development on cultural competence.

MATT

Speaking of additional things our group has been talking about— we want to create a survey of teaching styles for our staff. Since we have a better idea of students' learning styles, we need to understand how our teachers teach best and provide necessary professional development opportunities. We are working with State University to support these development needs.

Chris

Don't forget about our conversations with State University's admissions office. They want to work directly with our counseling office and with students in the classrooms to help students better understand how their experiences here can help support their success at the university.

Danita

Slow down, slow down. Getting the two of you together with a handful of data sure is dangerous!

Chris

We're excited! Isn't this what we are supposed to be doing? It always bothered me when people would say things like, "let's do what is best for kids." Now, I feel that we are actually doing tangible things that will make a difference.

Matt

I could not agree more. And you know what, it really feels good to have a partner in this. Leading can be lonely—especially when you are leading change. Having Chris working alongside me on this has made all the difference.

The End…but not really!

The process of transforming or generating school structures that might facilitate collective leadership begins by surveying the school landscape with multiple sources of data (Militello & Janson, 2008). What kinds of structures or procedures are already in place that may be ripe for transformation?

Our Change

A key aspect of the relationship between principals and counselors is the identification of pivotal structures and processes that can be transformed to better serve the school's mission. For us, several elements contributed to this, including a distributed leadership framework, collaboration and communication, engagement in actual practice, and the ability to transform structures.

Distributed Leadership Framework

The distributed leadership perspective has grown increasingly popular in recent years. Although distributed leadership has sometimes been positioned as a "cure-all" educational practice in schools, it is perhaps best viewed as a perspective for developing insights that can contribute to improved leadership practices, rather than a prescriptive "blueprint for doing school leadership more effectively" (Spillane, 2006, p. 9).

The distributed leadership perspective diverges significantly from more traditional views of leadership (i.e., a view of leadership as the unilateral actions of one powerful leader) by expanding the unit of analysis from individual action to the work of a multitude of actors bringing their expertise around specific tasks (Spillane, 2005). The distributed leadership perspective tells a new, more accurate story of real change. The main foci of this perspective is that leadership for change emerges through: (1) collaboration and communication between multiple people; (2) engagement in actual practice, e.g., actions aimed at meeting set goals; and (3) the ability to transform structures (Harris & Spillane, 2008).

As a result, we examine the dramatization through the distributed perspective—paying particular attention to the leadership interactions between two of the protagonists—Matt, the principal, and Chris, the school counselor.

Collaboration and Communication

Central to the distributed leadership perspective is the emphasis on leadership being a collaboration between two or more leaders (Spillane, 2006). Interdependent collaboration is the glue that binds the practices of leaders who may be working on the same aims or tasks either together or separately. The actual arrangements and allocations of leadership tasks are extended across the leaders involved in ways unique to each school and situation, but it is the interactions between those leaders that compose the essence of school leadership (Spillane, 2005). In this depiction, the interactions between Matt and Chris were both formal and informal, however, at the root of their collaboration were continual communication and arrangement of tasks based on the inherent context of the particular leadership activity.

Engagement in Actual Practice

One clear reframing in the distributed leadership perspective is the focus on how leadership occurs. Here, the focus is not on the leader as defined by role, but rather on actions informed by role (Spillane, 2005). That is, expertise of individuals is brought to bear around specific problems and/or tasks. This shift to leadership practices is important in key ways. It allows us to identify useful behaviors that can be distilled for future instructive use. Additionally, by focusing on leadership practices, the collaborative nature underlying them becomes clearer. Collaboration ensued because of commonality, not of the individuals, but of their work or tasks. In this case, the common goal of improving the referral process for students anchored new initiatives.

Ability to Transform Structures

Another key element of leadership exemplified within the portrayal here is the ability of leaders to work together in order to transform the form and function of existing school structures. Distributed leadership "presses us to consider organizational structure as more than a vessel for leadership activity" by emphasizing the interplay between these structures and the leaders who work within them (Spillane, Halverson, & Diamond, 2001, p. 26). By removing the students who challenged the home high school the most, school staff were able to avoid the difficult work of examining their own teaching and support practices.

Distributed Leadership and Relationships

Central to this dramatic depiction of leadership in action is the central role of the principal-school counselor relationship. In large part, it was through their collective interactions—distributed leadership practices—that change occurred. This "triumvirate" of collective leadership practices and the relationship between principals and school counselors are awareness, communication, and collaboration.

Awareness

Collective leadership practices are facilitated by strong relationships with a shared purpose and a vision centered on student achievement (Janson, Militello, & Kosine, 2008; Militello & Janson, 2007). However, principals and school counselors must be aware of their shared purpose and vision. By growing and nurturing awareness of common purposes and visions, principals and counselors can pool their collective skills, influence, and power in order to enact change.

An awareness of a common vision and purpose between pivotal school figures like principals and counselors also serves to strengthen the capacity within the school to identify, assess, and address persisting systemic barriers to student achievement. By pooling their expertise and views of students with capacity for data use in each position, the potential for using data to drive school reform is exponentially expanded.

Communication

The move from awareness to dialogue and mutual collaboration is essential and should not be left to chance or to the unpredictable variable of strong interpersonal relationships (Militello & Janson, 2007). As described earlier, a key to promoting collective leadership practices is the creation or transformation of structures in a school to make this happen (Militello & Janson, 2008). School principals and counselors often are in close physical proximity within schools. Such proximity often promotes the informal social interactions that can be vehicles for substantive discussions on school issues.

However, the dialogues between principals and counselors that occur around student achievement should not be left to occur solely through chance meanderings of less substance-laden conversations. They are too important. Thus, more formal structures that may serve as conduits for these important conversations must be in place (e.g., administrator-counselor retreats, regularly scheduled meetings, joint professional development workshops). Although Matt and Chris utilized their informal discourse to discuss school issues, they also recognized the importance of transforming certain staff meetings and establishing new ones in order to impact the inequitable referral process they identified in their school.

Collaboration

Professional collaboration between principals and school counselors entails breaking traditional barriers or silo-style expertise (Militello & Janson, 2007). That is, here two formerly separate professionals constantly communicate, share expertise, and construct new roles and practices—sometimes shared, sometimes separate, but always linked through common goals and visions.

Supporting Change and Transformation

Schools are charged with meeting students' emotional and cognitive learning, preparing a highly capable workforce, and developing conscious, informed citizens. Nonetheless, educators at all levels find great difficulties with the pluralities of their roles and responsibilities. Specifically, educators are not well-versed in the processes of inquiry and collaboration. If new norms of practice are to be realized, actors need to address very personal issues of their own practice. School principals and counselors are uniquely positioned to model such a process of collaborative inquiry. In this example, Matt and Chris demonstrated a willingness to interrogate and problematize not only systemic procedures within the school, but their own individual professional practices.

Next Steps

- **Formalize meetings between counselors and principals.** Principals should include counselors in meetings and vice versa. However, these meetings should have a clear focus on issues of teaching and learning. Adding operational meetings to either's calendar will have an opposite action.

- **Develop inclusive decision-making processes**. Decision-making bodies such as school improvement teams need to be expanded and developed for other focus areas of the school.

- **Scholarly collaboration.** Principals and counselors should seek out or generate opportunities to present together within and beyond the school. Such collaboration can further enhance their collective understanding of their shared purpose and their interdependent practices. Additionally, partnerships built around data-driven practices and school practitioner research might also lead to expanded understanding of their common goals.

- **Exploration of areas of role overlap**. Much might be learned from examining areas of overlap between the roles and functions of school counselor and principal. Such examinations might generate new approaches gleaned from the unique qualities of the others' respective professional training.

Conclusion

Only when staff become intentional about working in tandem do similarities become apparent. If the difference between serendipity and intent is "seeing" one another in their practice, then principals and counselors must create opportunities to see each other's work and to work in collaboration. Such axiomatic effects will impact the principal-counselor relationship and, more importantly, impact teaching and learning in a school.

Questions for Reflection

Principals and counselors, use the following questions for reflection:

1. Are your current practices in your school determined mostly by a role-based conception of your work or by the specific requirements of the tasks or activities that need to be accomplished?

2. How would you describe your current relationship with your counselor/principal?

3. What do you know about the work of your counselor/principal? What do you know about the professional training and standards of your principal/counselor? What do you need to know? How might you develop this understanding?

4. How might you work with your counselor/principal to develop a more collaborative or distributed approach for school tasks and activities?

5. What barriers currently exist that prevent more effective collaboration with your counselor/principal?

References

Harris, A. & Spillane, J. (2008). Distributed leadership through the looking glass. *Management in Education, 22*(1), 31-34.

Janson, C. (2008, Summer semester). EDF 6607, Education in America. Class lecture. University of North Florida.

Janson, C., Militello, M., & Kosine, N. (2008). Four views of the professional school counselor and principal relationship: A Q methodology study. *Professional School Counseling, 11*(6), 353-361.

Militello, M. (2007, Spring semester). Research in school leadership. Class lecture. University of Massachusetts at Amherst.

Militello, M. & Janson, C. (2007). Socially focused, situationally-driven practices: A study of distributed leadership among school principals and counselors. *Journal of School Leadership, 17*(4), 409-442.

Militello, M. & Janson, C. (2008, Summer semester). EDF 6607, Education in America. Class lecture. University of North Florida.

Spillane, J. P. (2005). Distributed leadership. *The Educational Forum, 69*(2), 143-150.

Spillane, J. P. (2006). *Distributed leadership*. San Francisco: Jossey-Bass.

Spillane, J. P., Halverson, R., & Diamond, J. B. (2001). Investigating school leadership practice: A distributed perspective. *Educational Researcher, 30*(3), 23-28.

Chapter 5

A Principal's Guide to Practical Considerations in the Organization and Management of the School Counseling Program

Ian Martin, Hilda Lopez, and John C. Carey

> " ...*What school counselors do or fail to do are*
> *key factors affecting the future of many students.*"
>
> —House & Hayes, 2002, p. 250

In the resource-limited world of public schools, every decision about a program positively or negatively affects another area of the system. Thus, maximizing a school counseling program's impact on student learning, development, and achievement should be a goal

Ian Martin, Ed.D., is an Assistant Professor in the Department of Counseling at the University of San Diego. Email imartin@sandiego.edu. Hilda Lopez, M.Ed., is the Director of Guidance and Counseling at the Socorro Independent School District in El Paso, Texas. Email hlopez06@sbcglobal.net. John C. Carey, Ph.D., is a Professor within the Student Development and Pupil Personnel Services Department at the University of Massachusetts, Amherst and the Director of the Center for School Counseling Outcome Research. Email jcarey@educ.umass.edu.

for both the principal and counselors—one that requires the art of organization and management. It is the proper organization and management of the program that supports implementation of the best possible interventions and activities. In addition, proper organization and management ensures that counseling program resources (e.g., counselor time, counselor focus, space, etc.) are employed in the most effective and efficient ways. This chapter focuses on the little details that can have a big impact on school counseling programs and, ultimately, the larger school environment.

In schools that aspire to achieve systemic reform of their school counseling programs, it is critically important to first assess the way the program is currently organized and managed. If the assessment reveals that the program design is one that has relegated the counselor to the role of "quasi-administrator" or "paperwork pusher," then the program organization and management should be changed. Without change, the best that can be hoped for is a temporary improvement in the program with an eventual backsliding into old habits. In this regard, it is particularly important to attend to the "nitty-gritty" of program organization and management (e.g., how counselors are hired, how students are assigned to counselors, what duties are assigned to counselors, etc.) because the decisions about these details will either liberate counselors to pursue best practices or constrain them to mediocrity.

However, despite the importance of this topic, very little research or comparative program evaluation data exists that would help guide decisions about program organization and management. Though there is literature describing best practices, it is largely based on collective knowledge and scattered across a number of disparate sources. The goal of this chapter is to summarize and evaluate this informed opinion about how best to organize and manage the school counseling program. We hope that providing guidance about effective program organization and management will help to demystify school counseling and allow principals to maximize the potential of innovative school counseling practices in their schools.

Is School Counseling a Program?

Before considering issues related to the structures and processes necessary for effective practice, it helps to consider whether school counseling is best considered a position or a program. If school counseling is a position, then management may simply mean hiring the right person for the job and ensuring that he or she does the job well. Typically, this involves working with students and responding effectively to crises as they arise. If school counseling is a program, it has its own goals that are integral to overall school goals, and it must be managed to ensure these goals are met.

A shift in this position or program concept has changed over time. Up until the 1980s, counseling in schools was conceptualized as a position responsible for providing a set of services to students. Accessing these services was typically based on the immediate needs of the campus. Thus, the school counselor operated in a reactive mode, although a few school counselors conducted periodic needs assessments to determine which services were most in demand. Evaluation of services was largely based on participation rates, student contacts, and (occasionally) "customer" satisfaction data.

Three factors led to the reconceptualization of school counseling as a program:

- First, innovations in the field led to an expanded range of services provided by school counselors. In addition to individual counseling services, school counselors began to deliver whole-school, classroom-based, and small-group interventions to students; consultation for teachers; and outreach and educational services for parents.

- Second, there was a broadening of school counseling's focus on addressing students' psychosocial, career, and academic development.

- Third, the importance of prevention was recognized, and counselors became more focused on delivering interventions in order to prevent: (1) the occurrence of problems in the general student population (primary prevention), (2) the development of specific problems in "at-risk" subpopulations (secondary prevention), and (3) nascent problems from becoming disabling problems in identified subgroups of students (tertiary prevention).

This broader spectrum of services—delivered to all students by a limited number of professionals—required the reconceptualization of school counseling as a program. It also required that school counselors manage competing needs systematically, set realistic program goals, and evaluate program outcomes.

The major model for school counseling programs is Comprehensive Developmental Guidance (CDG) (Gysbers & Moore, 1981). CDG maintains that the school counseling program should have its own curriculum and offer a mix of preventative-developmental and remedial services in a range of formats (whole-classroom interventions, group counseling, and individual counseling) so that all students receive the services they need. Since many schools, school districts, and state departments of education adopted CDG as their model for organizing and delivering school counseling services (Martin, Carey, & DeCoster, 2009; Sink & MacDonald, 1998), it can be considered fundamental to the practice of modern school counseling in the United States. Research supports the effectiveness of such a model with findings indicating that students benefit when services are organized and delivered in comprehensive developmental programs (Lapan, Gysbers, & Petroski, 2001; Lapan, Gysbers, & Sun, 1997; Sink & Stroh, 2003).

School counseling evolved still further over the last 20 years. Three noteworthy advances in school counseling practices were related to the *standards-based education reform* movement that has come to dominate public education:

- First, the Education Trust's Transforming School Counseling Initiative (Martin, 2002) reconceptualized the role of school counselors to emphasize their contribution to academic achievement and, in particular, their responsibilities related to eliminating systemic barriers that affect class- and race-related gaps in achievement. School counselors were seen as needing to use school data to identify and help eliminate problems—such as low expectations and inequitable school policies or practices—for the success of all students.

- Second, the American School Counselors Association (ASCA) developed a set of national standards that more clearly expressed the expected outcomes of school counseling programs in terms of students' academic, career, and personal social development (Campbell & Dahir, 1997).

- Third, ASCA also developed a *National Model for School Counseling Programs* that maintained the basic CDG principles of organizing and delivering services but added components designed to connect school counseling programs with standards-based educational reform (see Appendix A). Programs organized in accordance with ASCA national model standards adopt a variety of program management practices intended to ensure that they are focused on academic outcomes, connected to the academic mission of schools, use effective management practices, measure the impact of interventions on students, and are accountable for their outcomes (ASCA, 2005).

Despite the existence of these models, schools across the United States show great variability in how school counseling is practiced, organized, and managed. While over 40 state departments of education have developed models based on CDG and/or the ASCA National Model, these state models are typically neither mandated nor evaluated (Martin et al., 2009). In addition, under the principle of building-based management, many districts have delegated authority to school principals and left little authority with central-office-based guidance directors to determine school counseling practice. In other schools and districts, formal central-office direction over school counseling programs was never the norm.

Due to the existence of these arrangements, some building principals have responsibility for establishing the nature and organization of school counseling within their schools. Unfortunately, the vast majority of principals who ultimately define the work of school counselors and the nature of the school counseling program have little to no background in school counseling (Barret & Schmidt, 1986; Dollarhide, 2003). Specifically, few principals have had formal exposure to effective organization and management strategies for school counseling programs within either their initial licensure program or subsequent professional development. This reality requires that work be done to inform and aid principals in understanding the conditions, organization, and expectations that could lead to positive school counseling outcomes.

In response to this need, our intent here is to help school principals understand that school counseling is best considered a *program* with its own goals, activities, and evaluation practices. In line with this, the remainder of our chapter focuses on ways principals can support the establishment of a strong school counseling program and also develop realistic expectations for school counselors' work. Under such circumstances, counselors should be able to articulate the goals of the program, describe how these goals support the mission and goals of the school, and highlight how they know that program goals are being met.

How Many School Counselors Are Needed in the Program?

Although very little research is available on the proper staffing of school counseling programs, ASCA recommends a 250 to 1 ratio of students to counselors. Data from the National Center for Educational Statistics suggests that in the 2005-06 school year, the national average for high schools was 246 students per counselor and the national average for K-8 schools was 778 students per counselor, with large differences existing across states (NCES, 2008).

In general, it is safe to assume that a quality CDG-based program can be delivered in a school with student-to-counselor ratios of 250 to 1, but that does not mean that quality CDG programs cannot be delivered in schools exceeding this ratio. The important point to understand is that workable ratios create greater likelihoods that school counselors are able to provide a range of preventative and remedial services to all students. Workable ratios also enable counselors to provide consultative services to teachers and outreach and educational services for parents. And workable ratios allow counselors to coordinate services with teachers, collect data to monitor student progress, and evaluate their interventions and overall programs.

While a ratio of 250 to 1 is recommended, four important conditions need to be met that may be arguably more important than the student-to-counselor ratio:

- First, school counselors need to spend the bulk of their time (80% is generally recommended) on activities that benefit students. Often counselors are assigned by principals to noncounselor-related duties (e.g., bus duty, hall monitoring) that interfere with the delivery of comprehensive programs (Bemak, 2000; Burnham & Jackson, 2000; Gysbers & Henderson, 2000). Unfortunately, instances where the add-on duties comprise as much as 60% of a school counselor's time are not unusual.

- Second, counselors need to employ a range of intervention modalities to efficiently reach all students. These modalities include whole-school programs (e.g., bully prevention programs), classroom guidance, small groups, and one-on-one counseling. Many school counselors show an overreliance on one-on-one counseling and ignore more efficient ways to address needs.

- Third, many activities of the school counseling program require the collaboration of school counselors and teachers. For example, it may be more effective and efficient to incorporate school counseling program learning objectives into regular teacher-led classroom lessons in some cases. Having students learn how to write an effective essay focusing on their personal essay for college applications is a way to accomplish important academic and career-development objectives simultaneously. However, effective coordination between school counselors and teachers requires both administrative support and the joint planning time to develop lessons and materials.

- Fourth, the school counseling program requires clerical support, especially related to record keeping, scheduling, and correspondence. In many schools, clerical support is inadequate or nonexistent. School counselors are expected to perform both their professional work and the clerical work that supports it. In these instances, the time spent on clerical work reduces the time available for professional work.

Our collective knowledge and school-related experiences tell us that, if any student-to-counselor ratio is to be effective, counselors must spend the majority of their time on activities that benefit students, use a range of modalities to address problems, collaborate with teachers to share responsibility for fostering students' career and personal-social development, and have access to appropriate levels of clerical support. Principals and counselors should engage in a dialogue regarding each of these issues and talk about what assignments aid in meeting the objectives of a comprehensive program or are best left to other professionals, and how much clerical support is needed. There are many resources available to guide this activity (Gysbers & Henderson, 2000; Johnson & Johnson, 2003; Schmidt, 2003). For example, a time and task analysis (Fairchild & Seeley, 1994) is an objective and systematic way to take stock of how time is being used and an opportunity to explore alternatives.

What Are Effective Staffing Patterns?

Some elementary, most middle, and almost all high schools have more than one counselor associated with the program. This fact leads immediately to questions related to how the program work should be divided amongst the professional school counselors, with the key question being how the work should be organized to achieve program goals. No research currently exists to address these questions, so, again, we must rely on guidance from professional wisdom.

Most school counseling programs use some system for assigning students to counselors that creates roughly equal workloads. Most often this is an "alpha" approach—students are assigned to counselors based on the first letter of their last name, with roughly equal percentages of students assigned to each counselor. The primary purposes for assignment of students to counselors are that:

- counselors will know which students need to be monitored, and

- students and parents will know who to contact in the event that help or assistance is needed.

However, problems with this system may occur when students, parents, and/or counselors confuse their assignment or wish to make changes to their assignment (due to a myriad of student/counselor/parent-initiated reasons, such as personality conflicts, past family history, conflict of interest, etc.). To avoid such conflicts, we suggest that student assignments should not imply that a counselor only serves students on his or her caseload or that students and parents cannot seek help from another counselor. Counselors should not be sitting in their offices waiting for "their students" or "their parents" to make contact. Likewise, students or parents should not have to wait if "their counselor" is busy.

In addition, it is helpful to have a system that enables counselors to balance the time they need to be available for student-initiated and/or parent-initiated contacts with the time they need to spend implementing whole-school, classroom-based, and group interventions. One such "on-call" system has one counselor available at all times to handle crises and to see students and parents who need to be seen. Student "walk-ins" and parent "call-ins" have the option of seeing the on-call counselor immediately or making an appointment to see a counselor of their choice at the next open time. This on-call system adds needed flexibility to the alpha assignment, frees up counselors to do other types of work, and ensures that parents and students have choices and can access services in a timely manner.

Sometimes counselors are assigned to specific grade levels with students changing counselors when they are promoted to the next grade. Our experience has shown us that this organization can develop problems associated with both inequitable workload distribution and counselors' abilities to personally connect with students. For instance, high school counselors that are solely responsible for the senior class may spend an inordinate amount of time writing college recommendations for students they have just met. Thus, it is usually better to institute some form of "looping," where counselors follow students across grades to take advantage of the cumulative information they develop about students and establish relationships. A given counselor might start out with the first half of the ninth grade by alpha and follow these students through the next 4 years of high school.

In addition to assigning students to counselors, work may be distributed according to specializations. In these cases, different counselors have different responsibilities based on the specialized knowledge and skills needed to fulfill the responsibilities. In high schools, the most common specialization is college counseling. Here, the workload is often heavy and the specialized knowledge is complex. Often, college counselors do not have assigned students; this permits them to work with all students making the transition to college.

Other counselor specializations related to student transitions also have been found to be helpful. For example, some high schools have ninth-grade transition counselors who have the responsibility of coordinating and facilitating middle school students' (and their parents') transition to high school. This approach can prevent high-need students from falling through the cracks and help all students (and parents) adjust to changes in expectations, routines, and climates typical to transitioning from one school to another. Other high schools have specialized "school-to-work" or "career counselors" who handle students' transitions to work, including preparatory/ exploratory experiences and internships. Still other schools have counselors who specialize in adjustment or mental health counseling and work more intensely with students who have severe needs. Often, these counselors have a small assigned caseload and are expected to meet frequently with their students in one-on-one sessions to closely monitor progress and well-being.

One final approach to specialization deserves mention. Some schools have counselors who specialize in either career development, academic development, or psychosocial development. In addition to monitoring their assigned students, counselors are responsible for coordinating different aspects of the school counseling developmental curriculum. This system allows counselors to become experts in different aspects of the comprehensive prevention program. However, it requires a high level of coordination across counselors.

To review, a system that serves students and their parents, distributes the workload equitably, and takes maximum advantage of needed specializations will take on a different shape depending on the size/ level of the school and the needs of the school population. In general, it is best to:

- use alpha assignment to make sure all students and parents have a contact point and counselors know who they should be monitoring;

- use some form of looping to maximize continuity of contact; and

- establish specializations (e.g., college counseling, mental health counseling, ninth-grade transition counseling) that are related to the particular demands placed on the program or the goals of the program.

What Should Be Considered When Hiring A New School Counselor?

Hiring school counselors is a critically important task in building a strong program. Unfortunately, there is great variability in both quality and focus amongst school counselor preparation programs. Some programs have aligned the curriculum with current theory, research, and practice. Others have not. Some training programs see their mission as preparing mental health counselors to work in schools. Graduates of these programs may have strong skills in one-on-one therapeutic counseling, but may lack both the orientation and skills necessary to work in multiple modalities and to focus on prevention in addition to remediation. Similarly, there is great variability in the extent to which state licensure requirements are aligned with current theory, research, and practice (Martin et al., 2009). Unfortunately, then, having a diploma or holding a license does not guarantee that an applicant has the proper training and experience to work effectively in public schools. Great care must be taken in the hiring process to ensure that competent candidates are hired.

Good hiring decisions can be made if proper attention is paid to the fit between an applicant's skill set and dispositions and the nature of the work of a school counselor in a CDG program. It is critical that the screening and hiring process attends to applicants':

- training and skills in providing the array of services required in a CDG program (whole-school work, consultation skills, classroom guidance skills, group leadership skills, coordination skills, and individual counseling skills);

- positive disposition towards accountability;

- skill in evaluating interventions and the program;

- knowledge of the principles of effective organization and management of the school counseling program; and

- knowledge of the principles of effective schooling and school reform (including, for newer graduates, descriptions of the role of the school counselor from the perspectives of the Educational Trust Transforming School Counseling Initiative and the ASCA National Model).

In an attempt to help principals hire new school counselors who will be effective in their work, Beale and McCay (2001) made several suggestions that are summarized in Table 5.1. In their view, hiring requirements should be based on a current job description that accurately reflects the role and work of modern school counselors.

Kaplan and Evans (1999) present seven interview questions (see Table 5.2) designed to help a principal assess the extent to which an applicant has the knowledge, skills, and dispositions necessary for effective work in schools.

Table 5.1. Suggestions for Hiring Competent School Counselors
• Select counselors who can articulate their role in enhancing the success of all students.
• Search for counselors who can describe how they can contribute to curriculum development.
• Look for counselors who understand the counselor's role in school discipline.
• Enlist counselors who will serve as integral parts of the school's educational team.
• Seek applicants who have specific knowledge of special education procedures and interventions.
• Employ counselors who see working with families of all kinds as an important part of their jobs.
• Search for candidates who have demonstrated leadership in collaborating with the wider school community.
Source: Beale & McCay, 2001

Beale and McCoy (2001) recommend using a panel to screen applications and conduct screening interviews, with principals using "behavioral questioning" in the final interviews in order to identify the best applicant. Behavioral questioning aims to identify important skills and behavior patterns by asking for very specific information on past behavior. For example, a principal might ask "Can you please describe, in detail, the last time you were involved in an important decision regarding a child who was struggling in school. What were the circumstances, what did you do, and how did the situation turn out?"

> ## Table 5.2. Interview Questions Focusing on the School Counselors' Role in Promoting Achievement
>
> - Describe the role of the school counselor in the learning process.
> - What would you say if I asked you to take a leadership role in school improvement?
> - Describe how you would collaborate with teachers, students, and parents to support high achievement for all students.
> - How would you increase the academic achievement for all students, especially that of traditionally low-achieving students?
> - Describe your approach to career development for different grade levels.
> - What ideas do you have for communicating with parents?
> - In what areas are you working towards self-improvement?
>
> Source: Kaplan & Evans, 1999

What Factors Should Be Considered in the Selection of a School Guidance Director or Lead Counselor?

School guidance directors (head counselors or lead counselors) are counselors who have coordination and leadership responsibilities in the counseling program. In schools with four or fewer counselors, there may not be a need for a guidance director if the principal (or an assistant principal) is able to assume these responsibilities. However, with five or more counselors in a school, it is typically better to have one of the counselors take on responsibilities for program management.

A good guidance director is an experienced counselor who also has an understanding of how programs should be organized, managed, and evaluated. Leadership abilities and an understanding of the principles of CDG are essential. Knowledge of program planning, evaluation, and accountability practices is also critically important. Guidance directors must have the respect of both counselors and the teaching staff, and they must be able to forge strong working relationships with their principals.

The guidance director represents the counseling program within the school. He or she usually serves on the school leadership team and provides valuable perspectives based upon extensive interactions with a wide range of students, parents, and teachers, as well as familiarity with many types of student information. Guidance directors also need to be comfortable being the external representative of the program. Often, they prepare reports about the counseling program and may present these at school board meetings and other venues.

The guidance director typically supervises counseling program clerical support staff and usually provides input to the principal regarding the annual performance evaluation of school counselors. In addition, he or she often provides case consultation for other counselors, as well as special support to new counselors through their induction period. A guidance director should be evaluated annually by the principal based on performance both as a counselor and as program leader.

Hiring a Guidance Director

In the past, many states required that guidance directors be certified (beyond their initial certification as school counselors), and many universities offered certification programs for guidance directors that addressed the knowledge and competencies described above. Today, this is rare. Thus, it cannot be assumed that every school counselor has the knowledge and skills needed to function effectively as a guidance director, and the process of looking for qualified people may be a challenge. Obviously, it may be possible to hire a guidance director from outside the school or district. An alternative is to groom a school counselor for the position (apprenticing them to the current guidance director), so that he or she can develop the needed knowledge and experience base.

Whether a guidance director is hired from outside or selected from within, it is highly desirable that the selection process focus on the existence of or potential for learning the required skills in leadership, management, organization, collaboration, and evaluation—skills that distinguish the position from a regular school counseling position. Being a "master counselor" is not enough. Also, it is important to have both the principal and the school counselors involved in the selection process.

Effective Approaches for Supervising the Work of School Counselors

Another challenge for principals is the need to provide effective supervision for counselors. In regard to this, it is helpful to distinguish between two types of supervision—administrative and clinical—that counselors need.

Administrative supervision is typically the responsibility of the principal (although some facets of administrative supervision may be delegated to the guidance director) and involves directing and monitoring the work of the counselors, evaluating their performance, and providing any professional development that may be needed to remediate performance problems or enhance professional practice.

Quality administrative supervision requires an explicit mutual understanding of the nature of the work of school counselors and the relationship of the work to the goals of the program and school.

The ASCA National Model (ASCA, 2005) provides some help with the principal's role in regard to administrative supervision and suggests that annual principal-counselor agreements be developed at the beginning of each school year to identify the specific goals and responsibilities of counselors. Such agreements focus the work and establish specific program goals for the year. The discussion needed to develop them also provides an opportunity for the counselor and principal to talk about issues such as the percentage of time that will be allocated to each delivery system, the counselor's work schedule, professional development activities in which the counselor will participate, program goals, and services/programs that will be provided to parents, staff, and community.

In contrast, clinical supervision should not be the responsibility of the principal, since it requires specialized professional knowledge and skill in the discipline of school counseling. This type of supervision involves enhancing the capacity of counselors to do effective work with specific groups of individuals. Counselors need regular access to clinical supervision in order to find alternative ways to address problematic counseling situations and/or to add to their skill sets. Clinical supervision can be in a one-on-one or group format and can be thought of as a highly personalized, continuous form of professional development.

There is both data and a broad consensus that school counselors do not get enough clinical supervision nor do they recognize the need for additional supervision (Henderson & Lampe, 1992; Page,

Pietrzak, & Sutton, 2001), with this need especially evident in novice counselors. Access to clinical supervision seems to be limited by both a lack of tradition for this type of activity in schools and by a shortage of trained supervisors. However, it is unrealistic to think that a counselor could become proficient in complex interpersonal skills based solely upon the clinical supervision provided during initial training. There is a huge need within the field to increase the rationale for further supervision and create supervision solutions that fit the complex nature of schools.

Proficient counselors who can provide clinical supervision are not easily located. Supervisors need to be knowledgeable about the range of preventative and remedial work that characterizes comprehensive developmental programs, aware of effective models for the clinical supervision of school counselors (see Luke & Bernard, 2006; Wood & Rayle, 2006), and cognizant of the particular legal and ethical issues related to school counseling and school counselor supervision (see Herlihy, Gray, & McCollum, 2003).

Schools have utilized school counselors, guidance directors, central-office guidance supervisors, and community-based counselors (paid as consultants) to deliver clinical supervision services (Henderson & Lampe, 1992; Wilkerson, 2006). The effectiveness of this supervision depends on the knowledge and skills of the supervisor. Henderson and Lampe (1992) describe using guidance directors who received extra districtwide professional development training in the clinical supervision of school counseling as an effective model for delivering further supervision beyond initial training. Even though these guidance directors had a great deal of experience as school counselors, they still needed specific training in clinical supervision to function effectively in that other role.

Evaluation of Counselors

A sound performance evaluation system holds school counselors accountable for appropriate duties. Aligned with this should be sound administrative support and professional development to encourage professional growth. Good administrative supervision starts with a position description that accurately reflects the work of a school counselor in a comprehensive developmental program. For example, explicit addenda to this description should be made based on agreed-upon counselor specialization assignments (e.g., ninth-grade transition counseling, college transition counseling). Both the general work of a school counselor based on the district job description and the specific assignments of individual counselors ought to be explicitly outlined on a performance evaluation form.

An annual end-of-the-year performance evaluation meeting should be conducted with each counselor. In the meeting, the principal and counselor should review and discuss the principal-counselor agreement, performance data, the written feedback from the guidance director, and the principal's rating of the counselor on the performance evaluation form. After all performance evaluations are completed, the principal and guidance director should meet to determine the professional development needs of both individual counselors and the program as a whole.

How Can Principals Empower School Counselors to Become Leaders and Contributors to School Improvement?

A principal that practices "distributed leadership" and supports the creation of communities where the adults are engaged in continuous learning and improvement helps to enhance the capacity of all staff members in the school to educate all children (Elmore, 2000; Halverson, 2003; O'Day, 2004). School counselors have an important role to play in this school community.

The importance of school counselors pursuing a leadership role to promote systemic change in schools has been widely recognized (Herr, 2001; House & Hayes, 2002; Johnson & Johnson, 2003; Keys & Lockhart, 1999). There are several rationales presented as to why leadership is an essential school counselor trait. Podemski and Childers (1980) focus on features of the school counselor's role that position this person to help lead school improvement efforts:

- Counselors can usually take a systems perspective—seeing problems as resulting from the interaction of students with institutional characteristics and practices.

- Counselors typically have formal training in systemic analyses and also have a vantage point within the school that helps them see how all the groups and constituencies interact with each other.

- Relatedly, counselors have access to data and information (including confidential information) on student achievement and development from multiple sources. This helps them have access to the big picture and to then use their unique perspective to identify patterns that affect student learning and development.

- Counselors have expertise in child development and are recognized by teachers for this expertise.

- Most counselors are trained to identify policies and practices that impact students and suggest plausible, workable alternatives.

- Counselors also have formal training in program evaluation and know how to examine the outcomes of activities, practices, and policies.

- Counselors may have a more flexible schedule than classroom teachers, thus making it easier for them to schedule time to work with other professionals on school improvement efforts.

- Finally, counselors have good human relations skills that allow them to read the social interactions amongst school professionals and help move the "learning community" toward effective action. In this regard, it is an advantage that they have "staff authority" rather than "line authority" because they can influence their colleagues without threatening them.

Principals can take the best advantage of the unique perspective offered by school counselors by developing strong working relationships with them and by meeting frequently with the guidance directors or with a school counselor (in cases where there is no guidance director). Appointing a counselor to the school leadership team is a wise way to access valuable insights and information. Finally, appointing a school counselor to school task forces focusing on topics such as discipline or scheduling helps infuse a school counselor's larger perspective into discussions about essential school functions.

How Can Principals Support Collaboration Between Teachers and Counselors?

In some schools, counselors are seen as people who sit in their offices waiting to talk with students. In reality, however, this image fails to take advantage of an important resource. By teaming with others, counselors can help improve the organization and delivery of academic instruction. Principals ought to encourage opportunities for such interactions by supporting opportunities for collaboration between counselors and teachers. Table 5.3 contains some examples of effective counselor-teacher collaborations.

Table 5.3. Examples of Effective Counselor-Teacher Collaboration

- An elementary school counselor and a veteran teacher lead a weekly instructional improvement group for four novice teachers.
- An elementary school counselor and a teacher research, select, and implement a classroom-based bullying prevention program.
- A middle school counselor leads weekly group consultation sessions on managing problematic classroom behavior with the four teachers in a 100-student "house."
- A middle school counselor and a teacher meet with the high school's 9th-grade transition counselor to identify problematic transitions and plan solutions.
- A high school counselor serves as a liaison to academic departments in order to help the departments develop better policies on course sequences, course requirements, and honors requirements.
- A high school counselor develops a career decision-making curriculum with new 10th-grade teacher-advisors and provides training and materials on group leadership skills.
- A high school counselor and an English writing teacher codevelop a lesson plan that teaches essay writing using the college application essay format.

Teaming and collaboration typically require joint shuffling of schedules, workloads, and resources. Principals can facilitate counselor/teacher collaboration by creating a process for proposing opportunities for collaborative projects, allowing flexibility within work schedules, and supporting important proposals with modest funding for materials and stipend pay for after-school or summer work. Unleashing creative solutions to problems that can potentially emerge from such collaborations is worth the small investment that is required.

How Can Principals Encourage Effective Program Planning, Management, and Accountability?

ASCA (2005) suggests several useful ways to ensure that the counseling program is aligned with the school's goals and functionality. First, a program mission statement that is aligned with the school's mission and goals can provide focus and direction for program activities. Second, a program advisory board composed of key parents and teachers can help ensure that the needs and expectations of the school community are being addressed by the program. Third, principal-counselor agreements—reviewed annually and updated as necessary—can help identify goals that require immediate attention and action. Fourth, a master calendar that schedules the school year's preventative programs, groups, and important recurring activities can ensure that attention is paid to all the important aspects of the program rather than being reactively directed toward the "crisis of the day."

Fifth, accountability should be addressed. ASCA (2005) suggests that the counseling program ought to prepare yearly outcome reports that summarize the activities of the program and the results achieved. In addition, periodic program audits (every 5-7 years) should be done to evaluate the extent to which the program is achieving its major overarching goals and serving its constituencies. Results from both the annual evaluations and the less-frequent audits should be broadly disseminated to the various parties concerned with the counseling program and its impact.

The Los Angeles County Office of Education has developed a novel and effective one-page format for annual reports. The "Support Personnel Accountability Report Card" (SPARC) describes the school counseling program and documents its impact on students' learning and development (see http://www.sparconline.net/). Participating schools produce a SPARC report every year, and the county office presents awards to schools with exemplary report cards. Several hundred schools in California currently participate, and other states are in the process of implementing similar report cards. Having a yearly report that makes the accomplishments of the school counseling program visible to the school and the community is a great idea!

Adequate models and tools exist to support effective planning, management, and accountability. Principals should communicate their expectation that these models and tools be used, ensure that counselors get the necessary professional development and support to adopt these models and tools, and recognize that progress toward full implementation requires rigorous accountability structures.

Summary

Although optimizing the work of any staff member within a school requires commitment and concerted leadership, knowledge of the how-to's is important as well. This is especially true for school counseling—an area in which many principals received little preservice preparation. However, school principals are the key players in creating the structures that could enable school counseling programs to positively contribute to establishing healthy educational systems. This chapter was designed to guide principals through the "nitty-gritty" organizational and managerial structures that promote effective and efficient school counseling programs. We believe that paying close attention to these crucial factors is worthwhile and hope that these details spark interest in re-examining the ways in which school counseling is organized and managed in schools.

Questions for Reflection

Principals, use the following questions for reflection:

1. Is school counseling organized as a program or position within your school?

2. Who is responsible for overseeing school counseling within your school or district?

3. Are counselor-to-student ratios within your school or district workable? If not, what conditions could be addressed to make them more manageable?

4. How is school counselor work divided and/or organized within your school or district? Is it purposeful? Is it equitable? Does it involve opportunities for school counselor specialization?

5. How are school counselors hired within your school or district? What do you currently consider as critical school counselor qualities? Do they match what is advocated in the chapter?

6. How are school counselors supervised within your school or district? What opportunities can you identify that may provide further supervision and training beyond preservice supervision?

7. How are school counselors currently evaluated within your school or district? Are evaluation practices explicitly connected to both the development of the individual and the program as a whole?

8. What strategies can you identify to better access school counselors' unique perspective?

References

American School Counselor Association. (2005). *The ASCA National Model: A framework for school counseling programs.* Alexandria, VA: Author.

Barret, R., & Schmidt, J. (1986). School counselor certification and supervision: Overlooked professional issues. *Counselor Education and Supervision, 26,* 50-55.

Beale, A., & McCay, E. (2001). Selecting school counselors: What administrators should look for in prospective counselors. *Clearing House, 74*(5), 357-60.

Bemak, F. (2000). Transforming the role of the school counselor to provide leadership in education reform through collaboration. *Professional School Counseling, 3*(5), 323-31.

Burnham, J., & Jackson, C. (2000). School counselor roles: Discrepancies between actual practice and existing models. *Professional School Counseling, 4*(1), 41-49.

Campbell, C. A., & Dahir, C. A. (1997). *The national standards for school counseling programs.* Alexandria, VA: American School Counseling Association.

Carrell, S., & Carrell, S. (2006). Do lower student-to-counselor ratios reduce school disciplinary problems? *Contributions to Economic Analysis & Policy, (5)*1. Article 11. Retrieved from, http://www.bepress.com/bejeap/contributions/vol5/iss1/art11

Dollarhide, C. T. (2003). School counselors as program leaders: Applying leadership contexts to school counseling. *Professional School Counseling, 6*(5), 304-08.

Elmore, R. (2000). *Building a new structure for school leadership.* Washington, DC: Albert Shanker Institute.

Fairchild, T., & Seeley, T., (1994). Time analysis: Still an important accountability tool. *School Counselor, 41*(4), 273-80.

Gysbers, N. C., & Moore, E. H. (1981). *Improving guidance programs.* Englewood Cliffs, NJ: Prentice Hall.

Gysbers, N. C., & Henderson, P. (2000). *Developing and managing your school guidance program* (3rd ed.) Alexandria, VA: American Counseling Association.

Halverson, R. (2003). Systems of practice: How leaders use artifacts to create professional community in schools. *Educational Policy Analysis Archives, 11*(37), 1-35.

Henderson, P., & Lampe, R. E. (1992). Clinical supervision of school counselors. *The School Counselor, 39*, 151-157.

Herlihy, B., Gray, N., & McCollum, V. (2003). Legal and ethical issues in school counselor supervision. *Professional School Counseling 6*, 55-60.

Herr, E. L. (2001). The impact of national policies, economics, and school reform on comprehensive guidance programs. *Professional School Counseling, 4*, 236-245.

House, R., & Hayes, R. L. (2002). School counselors: Becoming key players in school reform. *Professional School Counseling, 5*, 249-256.

Johnson, S., & Johnson, C. D. (2003). Results-based guidance: A systems approach to student support programs. *Professional School Counseling, 6*, 180-184.

Kaplan, L. S., & Evans, M. W. (1999). Hiring the best school counseling candidates to promote students' achievement. *NASSP Bulletin, 83*(603), 34-39.

Keys, S. G., & Lockhart, E. (1999). The school counselor's role in facilitating multisystemic change. *Professional School Counseling, 3*, 101-107.

Lapan, R. T., Gysbers, N. C., & Petroski, G. F. (2001). Helping seventh graders be safe and successful in school: A statewide study of the impact of comprehensive guidance and counseling programs. *Journal of Counseling and Development, 79*, 320-330.

Lapan, R. T., Gysbers, N. C., & Sun, Y. (1997). The impact of more fully implemented guidance programs on the school experiences of high school students: A statewide evaluation study. *Journal of Counseling & Development, 75*, 292-302.

Luke, M., & Bernard, J. M. (2006). The School Counseling Supervision Model: An extension of the Discrimination Model. *Counselor Education and Supervision, 45*, 282-295.

Martin, P. J. (2002). Transforming School Counseling: A national perspective. *Theory Into Practice, 41*(3), 148-153.

Martin, I., Carey, J., & DeCoster, K. (2009). A national study of the current status of state school counseling models. *Professional School Counseling, 12*, 378-386.

National Center for Educational Statistics (2008). Table 1. Retrieved August 13, 2008, from http://nces.ed.gov and http://nces.ed.gov/pubs2007/pesenroll06/tables/table_1CT.asp

O'Day, J. (2004). Complexity, accountability, and school improvement. In S. H. Fuhrman & R. Elmore (Eds.), *Redesigning accountability systems for education* (pp. 15-46). New York: Teachers College Press.

Page, B. J., Pietrzak D. R., & Sutton, J. M. (2001). National survey of school counselor supervision. *Counselor Education and Supervision, 41*, 42-50.

Podemski, R. S., & Childers, J. H. (1980). The counselor as change agent: An organizational analysis. *The School Counselor, 27*(3), 168-174.

Schmidt, J. (2003). *Counseling in schools: Essential services and comprehensive programs* (4th ed.). Boston: Pearson Education.

Sink, C. A., & MacDonald, G. (1998). The status of comprehensive guidance and counseling in the United States, *Professional School Counseling, 2*, 88-94.

Sink, C. A., & Stroh, H. R. (2003). Raising achievement test scores of early elementary school students through comprehensive guidance and counseling programs. *Professional School Counseling, 6*(5), 350-365.

Wilkerson, K. (2006). Peer supervision for the professional development of school counselors: Toward an understanding of terms and findings. *Counselor Education and Supervision, 46*, 59-67.

Wood, C., & Rayle, A. D. (2006). A model for school counseling supervision, the Goals, Functions, Roles and Systems model. *Counselor Education and Supervision, 45*, 253-266.

Chapter 6

What Works in the Field: Comprehensive School Counseling Programs

Chris Janson and Carolyn Stone

The educational landscape of the 21st century presents an array of challenges and opportunities for principals and school counselors to renew their practice and respond to the climate of school reform. Voices from the profession have called for a shift in the role of the professional school counselor from that of individual service provider to one of promoting optimal achievement for all students in a comprehensive manner (Clark & Stone, 2007; Martin, 1998). Comprehensive school counseling programs provide principals with another resource to be used to impact student and school performance. They guide school counselors toward a standards-based approach arranged in a scope and developmental sequence with performance benchmarks. Student outcomes are primary data points focused on personal/social behavior, academic skills, and career proficiencies. Thus, the educational agenda of the school, school district, and society becomes the focus of the school counselor's role through a planned program that provides prevention and intervention.

Chris Janson, Ph.D., is an Assistant Professor of Counselor Education at the University of North Florida. Email c.janson@unf.edu. Carolyn B. Stone is a Professor of Counselor Education at University of North Florida. Email cstone@unf.edu.

Chapter 1 of this book presented information on the imperative for a comprehensive program and Chapter 5 provided the processes and practices to organize and manage the school counseling program, while Chapter 2 provided the rationale for school counselors to move to a data-driven school counseling program. It also provided guidance on how to assess whether the program is making a difference in the critical data elements found on school and school district report cards. This chapter answers the question, "What is happening in the field as schools implement a comprehensive school counseling program?" Case studies will be presented through the lens of systemic change, advocacy, and leadership.

This chapter is designed to help principals recognize the value of having a comprehensive school counseling program that is tied to helping all students and ensuring that they are all—not just the top 5% or the most at-risk students—given the support needed to become successful learners. To illustrate the critical elements of effective school counseling programs and the powerful impact these programs have on students and schools, this chapter highlights schools that have adopted the American School Counselor Association (ASCA) National Model designation, indicating the adoption of a comprehensive counseling program. Successful designees earn Recognized ASCA Model Program (RAMP) status, the professional gold standard in comprehensive school counseling program development.

Why Implement Comprehensive School Counseling in My School?

Given the myriad of challenges confronting school principals, they may understandably ask why they should accept yet another change to how their school addresses student needs. With certainty, shifts in professional practice do not occur easily. What, then, are the benefits of working to transform how school counseling is conceptualized and enacted from individual service providers to a comprehensive program? The short answer is that comprehensive, developmental, and results-based school counseling programs will make principals' job easier. They employ strategies to support student achievement and success, provide career awareness, open doors to opportunities, encourage self-awareness, foster interpersonal skills, and help all students acquire skills for life (Dahir, 2004).

Recent studies (Brigman & Campbell, 2003; Dimmitt, 2003; Galassi & Akos, 2004; Lapan, Gysbers, & Petroski, 2001; Sink & Stroh, 2003) have demonstrated the positive effects of comprehensive, developmental, and results-based school counseling on the academic achievement of elementary and secondary school students. This research suggests that high-quality counseling services can have long-term effects on a child's well-being and can prevent a student from turning to violence and drug or alcohol abuse. High-quality school counseling services can also impact a student's academic achievement. Studies on the effects of school counseling have shown positive effects on students' grades, reducing classroom disruptions, and enhancing teachers' abilities to manage classroom behavior effectively. Finally, high-quality school counseling services can help address students' mental health needs (U.S. Dept. of Education, 2002, p. 117).

Equity and Access as a Philosophical Underpinning of the Model

Not only is the ASCA National Model intended to be a blueprint to help school counselors design, implement, manage, and evaluate their own unique programs, but the model encourages the school counselor's role in the philosophical underpinnings of the Transforming School Counseling Initiative, which is to promote equity and access for all students by generating and supporting systemic change through applying leadership and acting as advocates for student success and opportunity (Martin, 2002). Equity and access means that school counselors are integral to ensuring that every child in their charge arrives at commencement prepared to chose from a wide range of postgraduation options, including attending a 4-year college.

Systemic stratification of opportunities connects the school counselor and the school counseling program to social justice advocacy and accountability with the expressed purpose of positively impacting equity, access, and success in rigorous coursework. The school counselors should always work toward answering the question, "How are students advantaged as a result of what we do?" (Education Trust, 1997). School counselors work intentionally with the expressed purpose of reducing the effect of the environmental and institutional barriers that impede student academic success (Stone & Dahir, 2004) and are in a unique position to exert a powerful influence (Clark & Stone, 2007; Stone & Clark, 2001). Thus, transformed school counselors build on the traditional practice of services and extend their skills by delivering comprehensive school counseling programs that are standards-based and data-driven. These skills, in the transformed context, are briefly reviewed with accompanying case examples extracted from programs that have applied for ASCA RAMP status.

The Role of the Counselor-Leader to Support Closing the Achievement Gap

Comprehensive school counseling programs are developed, enacted, coordinated, and measured using processes that are demanded from other educational programs. Similar in presentation to other programs in education, components include student outcomes or competencies, activities to achieve the desired outcomes, professional personnel, materials, resources, and a delivery system. These three approaches to program development show the connection of school counseling to the total educational process and, also, the need to involve all school personnel (Stanciak, 1995). These program approaches share common goals, are proactive and preventive in focus (Borders & Drury, 1992), and assist students in the acquisition of lifelong learning skills by:

- providing developmental, prevention, and intervention programs;

- measuring student and program growth; and

- taking into consideration the rapidly changing nature of society, as well as pressures on education from business and industry and how these impact every student's need to acquire academic, career, and personal-social growth and development (American School Counselor Association [ASCA], 2003).

The Emergence of Comprehensive School Counseling

ASCA borrowed heavily from comprehensive school counseling by Gysbers and Henderson (2000), the results-based approach of Johnson and Johnson (2002), the developmental model by Myrick (2003), and the sweeping impact on counselor preparation and public education called the Transforming School Counseling Initiative by the Education Trust (1997) to develop the ASCA National Model for comprehensive school counseling programs and set a new standard for practice by school counselors. To date, over 50,000 copies of the model have been distributed at the request of half of the approximately 100,000 school counselors in America.

The growing awareness of comprehensive school counseling programs, as seen through the acceptance of the ASCA National Model for comprehensive school counseling programs, is particularly remarkable when one considers just how differently school counselors were asked to view their work. The ASCA National Model requires a paradigm shift from working to support individual students in a reactive way, often ancillary to the educational mission of the school, to developing and coordinating a comprehensive program that involves administrators, other staff, parents, and community members who assist and guide implementation of a results-based program.

It should be noted that the ASCA National Model is intended to be just that—a model. It is not a monolithic template that is unresponsive to the idiosyncratic nature of schools and communities. ASCA itself is explicit on this matter, stating that "it is not meant to be replicated exactly," rather, each school and staff must "consider local demographic needs and political conditions" when developing their own programs. Although interpretations may vary, there is consensus that comprehensive, developmental, and results-based school counseling programs are systematic in nature, sequential, clearly defined, and accountable (ASCA, 2003; Galassi & Akos, 2004; Gysbers & Henderson, 2000; Johnson & Johnson, 1991, 2001; Johnson, Johnson, & Downs, 2006; Stone & Dahir, 2004; Stone & Martin, 2004). These skills, in the transformed context, are briefly reviewed, with accompanying case examples extracted from programs that have applied for ASCA RAMP status.

Case Examples

Southeast Raleigh Magnet High School, Raleigh, NC— Systemic Change

Southeast High School is an example of how a comprehensive school counseling program used data to identify and address academic inequity on a systemic level. The school counselors, in alignment with the district's goals, sought to increase the Advanced Placement (AP) enrollment of African American students. Rather than relying only on informal, anecdotal data, the school counselors examined disaggregated AP enrollment numbers in order to render the gap between the percentage of African American students enrolled in the school and the percentage of African American students enrolled in AP courses.

The counselors then collaborated with the building administrators to communicate that data to the content teachers. Simultaneously, the school counselors worked with the teachers and administrators in order to shift the AP enrollment criteria from student grade point average in their previous corresponding content courses to AP Potential Data (a statistical analysis based on PSAT scores). Additionally, the school counselors institutionalized AP Potential Parent Workshops—some specifically designed for African American students' parents and guardians—in order to build alliances with families so that both may be strengthened in their advocacy for students. Finally, the school counselors also implemented procedures for ensuring focused academic counseling promoting and supporting AP enrollment in a systematic way. As a result of their collaborative, systemic interventions, African American student enrollment in AP courses increased in 1 year from 94 to 151 students.

The systemic change highlighted in this case study points to the power of linking a multitude of interconnected systems to impact student success. Family, peers, the school, the community, and, sometimes, even the street within that community can influence their lives (Green & Keys, 2001; Keys, 2000; Littrell & Peterson, 2001). However, the alteration of the school system to support student success is the responsibility of all educators and, as a student advocate, the school counselor designs program collaboration and partnerships among stakeholders such as parents, educators and the community to move toward this goal (Lehr & Sumarah, 2002; Littrell & Peterson, 2001; Porter, Epp, & Bryant, 2000). Data-driven results are the key to linking school counseling programs to improved student success and levels of achievement. Measurable success resulting from this effort can be documented by an increased number of students completing school with the academic preparation, career awareness, and personal-social growth essential to choose from a wide range of substantial postsecondary options, including college (Education Trust, 1997). Without clearly connecting the practice of school counseling to its effects on students, the school counselor would remain conspicuously absent from conversations centered on reform efforts to promote higher levels of student success.

Ernesto Serna School, El Paso, TX—Advocacy

Ernesto Serna School is a dual-language K-8 school. In their RAMP application, the school counselors described their program as being "proactive" in serving the "long-term" needs of their students. In forward-tracking their students' performances and academic trajectories with staff at the feeder high schools, the school counselors identified a pronounced barrier for many of their students. When they reached high school, many of them needed opportunities to take additional core academic courses because they were non-English speakers. Counselors noted that, although these second-language learners were enrolled in both Spanish and English language arts courses in both the seventh and eighth grades, they received only one credit toward the two foreign language credits required for graduation in the state. Recognizing the advantages of granting two full credits (thus fulfilling state graduation requirements) for their Ernesto Serna coursework, the school counseling program successfully lobbied for policy change. The anticipated ramifications of that change were an increase in graduation rates for native Spanish-speaking students and enhanced academic preparation as a result of the opportunity for additional coursework in core academic areas.

Among the practices re-envisioned by the Transformed School Counseling Initiative was the notion that advocacy should center on access and support for all students, but particularly for students who have been traditionally underserved in our nation's schools (Martin, 2002). As seen in the case study, transformed school counseling programs seek to extend advocacy efforts beyond individual students to the systems of schooling themselves. Thus, new emphasis is placed on systemic interventions that might serve to change school structures and processes so that they might remove impediments and create opportunities for all students to reach their full academic potential through access to rigorous curriculum and high-quality teaching.

Baileywick Elementary, Raleigh, NC—Leadership

School leadership that produces substantial school change generally includes collaboration and communication with other staff, engagement in goal-oriented practices, and the ability to make new uses out of pre-existing programs or processes (Harris, 2008). As part of their comprehensive program at Baileywick Elementary, the school counselor demonstrated that her leadership embodied these elements. As the sole school counselor, she shared leadership on two instrumental school teams: the Student Services Team and the School Improvement Planning Core Team. Through her collaborative efforts with other staff on these two teams, she was able to ensure that her expertise and specialized school counselor training and content knowledge—including domains such as group processes, multicultural awareness and competence, and interpersonal communication—could be applied to the needs of the students and the school.

In addition to her involvement with these teams, she also took the lead in activities that promoted safety and character-building. Some of these activities included organizing ongoing, schoolwide training for the staff on violence prevention and social skills building; the development and administration of a student recognition program; the generation and maintenance of a character enrichment resource library; and cowriting a grant that supported cultural outreach to immigrant and noncitizen families.

Transformed school counseling leadership seeks ways to apply the language of educational reform and school improvement to school counseling programs. Transformed school counseling leadership does not exist in isolation, rather it encompasses shared practices in which multiple leaders work collaboratively to help ensure that all students gain access to information, curriculum, and opportunities that might allow them to achieve at higher levels (Janson, Clark, & Stone, in press). Through collaborative leadership, school counselors working through a comprehensive program with other educational staff and stakeholders are better equipped to generate and support systemic changes (House & Sears, 2002).

Lebanon High School, Lebanon, PA— Change in Service/Delivery

Essential to the shift from school counseling as an all-too-often isolated position to a comprehensive program is the notion that the school counselor is not solely responsible for the delivery of school counseling curriculum and services. This shift is parallel to the reciprocal notion that school counseling curriculum is not ancillary and alien to core academic content, but in many places, it overlaps with or complements it. In these respects, Lebanon High School is an exemplar. Through collaboration with the English Department, guidance curriculum is delivered to all students in grades 9-11. As their school counselors describe it, the lessons are incorporated into regularly scheduled English classes, often in alignment with assignments in those courses. Additionally, the lessons are sometimes taught solely by the school counselors and sometimes solely by the English teachers, but most often in teams. Additionally, because many of their activities and lessons involved technology, the collaboration also includes the school's media specialist and computer services personnel.

Chestnut Charter Elementary School, Dunwoody, GA— Change in Management

At Chestnut Charter Elementary school, the school counselor recognized the importance of establishing a Guidance Advisory Committee as a mechanism to not only deepen accountability to other school stakeholders, but also to expand the collective knowledge of the function and potential impact of comprehensive counseling programs. The school counselor noted that the establishment of the committee was the "first major step in advocating for the program." The committee included teachers, parents, and a local school board member who could then serve as a conduit to the remaining board members. The counselor noted that the spirit of collaboration engendered on the committee served to legitimize the conceptual and practical transition of school counseling from a position to a program responsive to the concerns and needs of the broader school and constituent communities. Additionally, components of the management system ensured that planning and goal setting was collaborative, a timeline was established for the delivery of services and programs, and the program was aligned with the school counseling standards and goals of school improvement.

Cibola High School, Albuquerque, NM— Accountability to Improve Outcomes

The school counseling program at Cibola High School embraced data for accountability purposes to improve outcomes for students. Through the development, implementation, and analysis of the resultant data from a needs assessment, the school counselors worked with the principal to make substantial changes in the school. Their needs assessment indicated that the vast majority of the students in the school desired more help in the area of career development. As a result of this schoolwide student assessment, the school counselors began working within existing school leadership structures, such as the steering committee, to radically alter student schedules in order to better meet student needs. As a result, the school moved from a six-period day to an eight-period day, and, in the process, provided each student with opportunities to take additional coursework directly related to career pathways of their choice. Additionally, the school counselors and administrators formed a robust alliance with the community college system in order to greatly expand the free concurrent enrollment program. Finally, the school began to infuse its subject-area curricula with opportunities to explore career options related to each area. As a result of these changes, the counseling program and the school feel strongly that students' postgraduation opportunities will be greatly enhanced, whether students are college-bound or directly entering the world of work.

Counselors Impacting Student and School Achievement

School counselors share responsibility to improve student learning and academic success, as well as to implement strategies to narrow the achievement gap. When school counselors work with the same school-based data as their colleagues, they share accountability for student outcomes and contribute to moving critical data (e.g., attendance rate, test scores, graduation rate, high school promotion rate, postsecondary enrollment rates, etc.) in a positive direction. The accountability system includes:

- alignment with the school improvement process
- using data to inform program development
- MEASURE tool (see Appendix B)

A successful school counseling program affords principals an additional resource to impact student outcomes. Counselors can measure effectiveness of services, demonstrate the benefits and impact of those services, or identify ways in which the services can be improved. Each year, school counseling programs set measurable goals in the academic, career, and personal-social development domains based on data, school improvement plans (SIP), and collaboration with school and community stakeholders. To evaluate the program and demonstrate accountability, school counselors must collect and use data that link the program to both student achievement and school improvement. School counselor accountability includes measurement, data collection, decision making, and evaluation focusing on student achievement and contributing to the school and district improvement goals.

Summary

Comprehensive school counseling programs reallocate the foci of school counselors so that their practices align with the educational agenda of the school, school district, and society. In doing so, comprehensive school counseling programs embody the response of the school counseling profession to the accountability-focused educational landscape in our era of school reform. This conceptual shift in school counseling from individual service providers to systematic, comprehensive, and accountable delivery of a standards-based approach with measurable student outcomes contributes to the educational mission of schools.

The value of having a comprehensive school counseling program is that, once it is designed and implemented, it can better support all students to be successful learners, without leaving any students behind. While there is little doubt that this conceptual transition is a significant one, there is also little doubt that it is one that is occurring with great frequency nationwide. To date, a vast number of schools have implemented effective school counseling programs—a handful of which have been highlighted here—and they are having a powerful impact on students and schools. These school counseling programs are emphatically demonstrating that their impact can extend far beyond the walls of the school counseling department into the total school practices, policies, and procedures, while injecting both with a greater commitment to educational equity and access for students.

Questions for Reflection

The process of implementing a comprehensive school counseling program is one that requires collaboration among all staff. In order for such a process to occur, thoughtful dialogue and important questions need to be explored as a staff. These questions represent a starting point in which principals and counselors can share in the task of engaging the school, students, and community in conversation that might lead to vital action toward the development of a school counseling program.

1. How have societal and educational changes impacted the needs of students in our school?

2. How are we as a school equitably and effectively addressing the academic and career planning needs of our students?

3. What are our individual and collective understandings of comprehensive school counseling programs and the roles, skills, and practices of school counselors within them as defined and described by the ASCA and the Transformed School Counseling Initiative?

4. In what ways do our academic content areas overlap with student standards and competencies as delineated by the ASCA?

5. How can our school counseling services better align with the educational needs of our students and the academic mission of our school?

6. How can we as school staff members, both individually and collectively, support the transition toward developing and implementing a comprehensive school counseling program?

7. What are impediments in our school to the development and implementation of a comprehensive school counseling program?

8. What are the assets and strengths in our school that might facilitate the development and implementation of a comprehensive school counseling program?

9. What are additional resources our school may need in order to continue toward developing and implementing a comprehensive school counseling program?

10. How might our students be different as a result of having a comprehensive school counseling program?

References

American School Counselor Association (2003). *American School Counselor Association National Model: A framework for school counseling programs.* Alexandria, Va: Author.

Borders, D. L., & Drury, R. D. (1992). Comprehensive school counseling programs: A review for policy makers and practitioners. *Journal of Counseling and Development, 70,* 487-498.

Brigman, G., & Campbell, C. (2003). Helping students improve academic achievement and school success behavior. *Professional School Counseling, 7,* 91–99.

Clark, M., & Stone, C. (2007). The developmental school counselor as educational leader. In J. Wittmer & M. Clark (Eds.), *Managing your school counseling program: K-12 developmental strategies* (3rd ed.). Minneapolis, MN: Educational Media Corporation.

Dahir, C. (2004). Supporting a nation of learners: The role of school counseling in educational reform. *Journal of Counseling and Development, 82*(3), 344-353.

Dimmitt, C. (2003). Transforming school counseling practice through collaboration and the use of data: A study of academic failure in a high school. *Professional School Counseling, 6*(5), 340-349.

Education Trust. (1997). *Working definition of school counseling.* Washington, DC: Author.

Galassi, J., & Akos, P. (2004). Developmental advocacy: Twenty-first century school counseling. *Journal of Counseling and Development, 82,* 146-157.

Green, A., & Keys, S. (2001). Expanding the developmental school counseling paradigm: Meeting the needs of the 21st century student. *Professional School Counseling, 5*(2), 84-95.

Gysbers, N. C., & Henderson, P. (2000). *Developing and managing your school guidance program* (3rd ed.). Alexandria, VA: American Counseling Association.

Gysbers, N. C., & Henderson, P. (2001). Comprehensive guidance and counseling programs: A rich history and a bright future. *Professional School Counseling, 4,* 246-256.

Harris, A. (2008). *Distributed school leadership: Developing tomorrow's leaders.* New York: *Routledge.*

House, R., & Sears, S. (2002). Preparing school counselors to be leaders and advocates: A critical need in the new millennium. *Theory Into Practice, 41*(3), 154-162.

Janson, C., Clark, M. A., & Stone, C. (in press). Stretching leadership: A distributed perspective for school counselor leaders. *Professional School Counseling.*

Johnson, S., Johnson, C., & Downs. L. (2006). *Building a results-based student support program.* Boston: Houghton Mifflin.

Johnson, C. D., & Johnson, S. K. (1991). The new guidance: A system approach to pupil personnel programs. *CACD Journal, 11,* 5-14.

Johnson, C. D., & Johnson, S. K.. (2001). *Results-based student support programs: Leadership academy workbook.* San Juan Capistrano, CA: Professional Update.

Johnson, C. D., & Johnson, S. K. (2002). *Building stronger school counseling programs: Bringing futuristic approaches into the present.* Chicago: Caps Publishers.

Keys, S. G. (2000). Living the collaborative role: Voices from the field. *Professional School Counseling, 3*(5), 332.

Lapan, R. T., Gysbers, N. C., & Petroski, G. (2001). Helping seventh graders be safe and successful: A statewide study of the impact of comprehensive guidance programs. *Journal of Counseling and Development, 79,* 320–330.

Lehr, R., & Sumarah, J. (2002). Exploring the vision: The comprehensive guidance and counseling program. *The School Counselor, 5,* 292-297.

Littrell, J. M., & Peterson, J. S. (2001). Transforming the school culture: A model based on an exemplary school counselor. *Professional School Counseling, 4,* 310-319

Martin, P. (1998). *Transforming School Counseling.* Unpublished manuscript. Washington, DC: The Education Trust.

Martin, P. (2002). Transforming school counseling: A national perspective. *Theory into Practice, 41*(3), 148-153.

Myrick, R. D. (2003). Accountability: Counselors count. *Professional School Counseling 6*(3), 174-179.

Porter, G., Epp, L., & Bryant, S. (2000). Collaborating among school mental health professions: A necessity, not a luxury. *Professional School Counseling, 3*(5), 315.

Sink, C. A., & Stroh, H. R. (2003). Raising achievement test scores of early elementary school students through comprehensive school counseling programs. *Professional School Counseling, 6,* 352–364.

Stanciak, L. (1995). Reforming the high school counselor's role: A look at developmental guidance. *NASSP Bulletin, 79,* 60-68.

Stone, C., & Clark, M. (2001). School counselors and principals: Partners in support of academic achievement. *National Association of Secondary School Principals Bulletin, 85(624),* 46-53.

Stone, C., & Dahir, C. (2004). *School counselor accountability: A measure of student success* (1st ed.). Upper Saddle River, NJ: Pearson Education, Inc.

Stone, C., & Martin, P. (2004). Data driven decision-makers. *ASCA School Counselor, 4* (3). 10-17.

U.S. Department of Education. (2002.) *No Child Left Behind: A desktop reference.* Washington, DC: Author.

Chapter 7
Where Do We Go From Here?

Chris Janson and Matthew Militello

Putting It All Together

As described from various vantages in the preceding chapters, effective partnerships between a school principal and counselor can not only enhance the individual work of both educators, but, most importantly, can serve as a synergistic, shared leadership core from which the tough work of school improvement and raising academic achievement can be better undertaken. Much of this book details specific content that comprises and enables school principal and counselor collaboration. For example, the content of specific schoolwide initiatives such as partnering around data use, collaborating with intention to address systemic barriers to student achievement, and using technology to facilitate collaboration are invaluable. However, the specific *content* tied to the educational mission of the school must be considered, along with the interpersonal *context* of principal and counselor collaboration (Janson, Militello, & Kosine, 2008). The relationship between the content on which

Chris Janson, Ph.D., is an Assistant Professor in the Department of Leadership, Counseling and Instructional Technology at the University of North Florida. Email c.janson@unf.edu. Matthew Militello, Ph.D., is an Assistant Professor of Educational Leadership and Policy Studies at North Carolina State University. Email matt_militello@ncsu.edu.

principals and counselors practice collaboratively and the interpersonal context of their relationship is a complex one that requires further study (Militello & Janson, 2007). However, there is little doubt that the relationship between the school principal and counselor is an important one and that the presence of an effective professional relationship is often accompanied by a tighter, more intentional school focus on the common educational mission. Thus, by examining elements of effective school principal and counselor relationships, we can begin to identify ways in which all principal and counselor relationships can be enhanced to greater effectiveness.

Eight Elements of Effective School Counselor-Principal Relationships

1. **Mutual value.** The principal and school counselor value each other's job responsibilities, tasks, and contributions to the school and its educational mission.

2. **Open and reflective communication.** The principal and school counselor are accessible and available to each other in order to discuss issues related to their individual or shared roles in the school, as well as issues relevant to the educational mission of the school.

3. **Shared belief in interdependency.** The principal and school counselor believe that many aspects of their individual roles cannot be accomplished without contributions from the other.

4. **Trust.** The principal and school counselor trust one another to support their own individual practices as well as their individual contributions to the shared educational mission of the school.

---

5. **Collective enterprise.** The principal and school counselor share in facilitating the development of the common educational mission of the school.

6. **Awareness of the other's repertoire.** The principal and school counselor understand each other's scope of training and professional expectations and standards.

7. **Purposeful and focused collaboration.** The principal and school counselor collaborate with intention around specific goals and strategies related to the common educational mission of the school.

8. **Stretched leadership.** The principal and school counselor share in leadership tasks and practices related to meeting the educational mission of the school.

Source: Janson & Militello, 2009

The Eight Elements of Effective School Principal-Counselor Relationships

The Eight Elements of Effective School Principal-Counselor Relationships evolved from a study we conducted in 2007 investigating how school counselors and principals perceived their current professional relationships with each other. In order to tie the research as closely as possible to the viewpoints and attitudes of the practicing school counselors and principals, we selected a method that allowed the subjectivity of working school principals and counselors to be paramount throughout the research process (Militello & Janson, 2007). From this study, four statistically distinct perspectives on the school counselor-principal relationship were identified and described (Janson, Militello, & Kosine, 2008). We also examined each of these perspectives through a conceptual framework involving how leadership is distributed in schools. Of the four, three represented positive incarnations of the relationship, while one seemed to embody a negative case. We learned a lot about the principal-school counselor relationship from each of these perspectives, whether their expressions of the relationship were positive or negative.

From our analysis of the perspectives on the school principal-counselor relationship in our study, we identified and derived eight elements of effective school principal-counselor relationships. These elements were present in at least one of the three perspectives of the relationship that were inherently positive, and absent from the more negative perspective.

Moving Toward More Effective Relationships in Your School

The Eight Elements of School Principal-Counselor Relationships resonate throughout this book. Collectively, the authors highlighted important practices, methods, and means that can help move school principals and counselors toward the generation and maintenance of more effective working relationships. While doing so, the authors also discussed or alluded to essential relational elements delineated in the Eight Elements (Janson & Militello, 2009). That is, much of the subtext of each of the chapters here highlight the importance of mutual value, open and reflective communication, a shared belief in interdependency, trust, a sense of collective enterprise, awareness of the other's repertoire, purposeful and focused collaboration, and stretched leadership. It is our hope that this book will serve at least two primary purposes. First, we believe that it can provide you with an opportunity to learn more about the powerful potential that effective principal-counselor relationships hold for being the epicenter of schoolwide improvement, reform, and transformation. Second, we believe that it can serve as a catalyst for you to engage with your counselor or principal counterparts in order to optimize your professional relationship while generating and clarifying the focus and purpose of your relationship around schoolwide educational initiatives.

Acknowledgments of Other Key Fellow Contributors

Knowledge does not emerge from a void. Likewise, research and theory do not develop apart from the meaningful contributions of others. As just two threads in the rich tapestry of scholarship on the important school counselor-principal relationship, we feel obligated by profession and out of deep respect to acknowledge those whose fine work contributed to both our interest in this topic and our thinking about it. With the caveat that the generation of lists such as this is always perilous in that we will invariably and unintentionally leave some important contributors out, in addition to our fellow contributors in this book, we would like to recognize the following scholars: Ellen Amatea, Victor Ballestero, Barbara Brock, Mary Ann Clark, William Cleveland, Colette Dollarhide, Jennifer Donegan, Trey Fitch, Gary Goodnough, Lynne Guillot Miller, Candice Jones, Matthew Lemberger, Jennifer Marshall, Jason McGothlin, Earl Newby, Katherine Niebuhr, Robert Niebuhr, Rachelle Perusse, Debra Ponec, Marie Shoffner, Alexandria Smith, and Robert Williamson.

References

Janson, C., & Militello, M. (2009). *Are we there yet? Factors that foster and inhibit urban school counseling reform.* Paper presented at the annual conference of the American Educational Research Association Annual Conference, San Diego, CA.

Janson, C., Militello, M., & Kosine, N. (2008). Four views of the professional school counselor and principal relationship: A Q methodology study. *Professional School Counseling, 11*(6), 353-361.

Militello, M., & Janson, C. (2007). Socially focused, situationally driven practices: A study of distributed leadership among school principals and counselors. *Journal of School Leadership, 17*(4), 409-442.

Appendix A

The ASCA National Model: A Framework for School Counseling Programs[2]

The American School Counselor Association National Model consists of four interrelated components: foundation, delivery system, management systems and accountability. The first component, foundation, dictates how the program is managed and delivered, which in turn, leads to the accountability of the program. The information gathered through the accountability process should refine and revise the foundation. Infused throughout the program are the qualities of leadership, advocacy and collaboration, which lead to systemic change.

Historically, many school counselors spent much of their time responding to the needs of a small percentage of students, typically those who were high-achievers or who were high risk. ASCA's National Model outlines a program allowing school counselors to direct services to every student.

As educators who are specially trained in childhood and adolescent development, school counselors can take a leadership role in effecting systemic change in a school. However, a successful school counseling program is a collaboration of parents, students, school counselors,

---

2 Excerpted from Executive Summary of the ASCA National Model: A Framework For School Counseling Programs, American School Counselor Association, http://www.ascanationalmodel.org/.

administrators, teachers, student services personnel and support staff working together for the benefit of every student.

The ASCA National Model: A Framework for School Counseling Programs keeps the development of the total student at the forefront of the education movement and forms the needed bridge between counseling and education.

Foundation

Like any solid structure, a school counseling program is built on a strong foundation. Based on the school's goals for student achievement, what every student should know and should be able to do, the foundation determines how every student will benefit from the school counseling program.

Beliefs and Philosophy—The philosophy is a set of principles guiding the program development, implementation and evaluation. All personnel involved in managing and implementing the program should reach consensus on each belief or guiding principal contained in the philosophy.

Mission—A mission statement describes the program's purpose and goals. A school counseling program mission statement aligns with and is a subset of the school and district's mission.

Delivery System

Based on the core beliefs, philosophies and missions identified in the foundation, the delivery system describes the activities, interactions and methods necessary to deliver the program.

Guidance Curriculum—The guidance curriculum consists of structured developmental lessons designed to assist students in achieving the desired competencies and to provide all students with the knowledge and skills appropriate for their developmental level. The guidance curriculum is infused throughout the school's overall curriculum and is presented systematically through K-12 classroom and group activities.

Individual Student Planning—School counselors coordinate ongoing systematic activities designed to assist students individually in establishing personal goals and developing future plans.

Responsive Services—Responsive activities are provided to meet individual students' immediate needs, usually necessitated by life events or situations and conditions in the students' lives. These needs require counseling, consultation, referral, peer mediation or information.

Systems Support—Like any organized activity, a school counseling program requires administration and management to establish, maintain and enhance the total counseling program.

Management System

Intertwined with the delivery system is the management system, which incorporates organizational processes and tools to ensure the program is organized, concrete, clearly delineated and reflective of the school's needs. This is a relatively new concept for administrators and school counselors who traditionally have not viewed counselors as "managers."

Agreements—Management agreements ensure effective implementation of the delivery system to meet students' needs. These agreements, which address how the school counseling program is organized and what will be accomplished, should be negotiated with and approved by designated administrators at the beginning of each school year.

Advisory Council—An advisory council is a group of people appointed to review counseling program results and to make recommendations. Students, parents, teachers, counselors, administration and community members should be represented on the council.

Use of Data—A comprehensive school counseling program is data driven. The use of data to effect change within the school system is integral to ensuring every student receives the benefits of the school counseling program. School counselors must show that each activity implemented as part of the program was developed from a careful analysis of students' needs, achievement and/or related data.

Action Plans—For every desired competency and result, there must be a plan outlining how the desired result will be achieved. Each plan contains:

1. competencies addressed
2. description of the activity
3. data driving the decision to address the competency
4. timeline in which activity is to be completed
5. who is responsible for delivery
6. means of evaluating student success
7. expected results for students

Use of Time—ASCA's National Model recommends that school counselors spend 80 percent of their time in direct service (contact) with students and provides a guide to school counselors and administrators for determining the amount of time their program should devote to each of the four components of the delivery system. Because resources are limited, school counselors' time should be protected; duties need to be limited to program delivery and direct counseling services, and non-counseling activities should be reassigned whenever possible.

Use of Calendars—Once school counselors determine the amount of time necessary in each area of the delivery system, they should develop and publish master and weekly calendars to keep students, parents, teachers and administrators informed. This assists in planning and ensures active participation by stakeholders in the program.

Accountability

School counselors and administrators are increasingly challenged to demonstrate the effectiveness of the school counseling program in measurable terms. To evaluate the program and to hold it accountable, school counselors must collect and use data that link the program to student achievement.

Results Reports—Results reports, which include process, perception and results data, ensure programs are carried out, analyzed for effectiveness and modified as needed. Sharing these reports with stakeholders serves to advocate for the students and the program. Immediate, intermediate and long-range results are collected and analyzed for program improvement.

School Counselor Performance Standards—The school counselor's performance evaluation contains basic standards of practice expected of school counselors implementing a school counseling program. These performance standards should serve as both a basis for counselor evaluation and as a means for counselor self-evaluation.

Program Audit—The primary purpose for collecting information is to guide future action within the program and to improve future results for students.

Appendix B

MEASURE

Mission, Element, Analyze, Stakeholders-Unite, Results, Educate:

A Six-Step Accountability Process for School Counselors

Name of School:_____

Principal: _____

Name of Counselor(s) Leading the Initiative: _____

Enrollment: _____

School Demographics (include percent of students in each category):

Caucasian/Non-Hispanic	_____ %
African American	_____ %
Hispanic	_____ %
Asian/Pacific Islander	_____ %
Native American	_____ %
Multiracial	_____ %
Free/reduced price lunch	_____ %
English Language Learners	_____ %
Exceptional Student Education/Special Education	_____ %

STEP ONE—MISSION: Connect your work to your school's mission in keeping with the ASCA or your state's comprehensive school counseling model.

Your school or department's mission statement is: _____

_____

_____

STEP TWO—ELEMENT: What critical data *element* are you trying to impact? (Examples include grades, test scores, attendance, promotion rates, graduation rates, postsecondary going rate, enrollment into honors or AP courses, special education, discipline referral data, and so on.) What is the *baseline* for the data element? Where do you hope to move it (*goal*)?

Element:_____

Element Baseline: _____

Goal: _____

STEP THREE—ANALYZE: Analyze the data element. You can use percentages, averages, raw scores, quartiles, or stanines. You can aggregate or disaggregate the data to better understand which students are meeting success. You can disaggregate by gender, race, ethnicity, socioeconomic status, or in a multitude of ways to look at student groupings.

The baseline data revealed: _____

_____

STEP FOUR—STAKEHOLDERS-UNITE: Identify strategies intended to impact the data element that will be used by any of the people/groups involved. Also identify the beginning/ending date of the overall effort.

Beginning date:_____ Ending date:_____

Stakeholders	Strategies
School counselor(s)	
Administrator(s)	
Teachers	
Classroom teacher assistants	
Other support staff (front office, custodial, cafeteria, playground)	
School Improvement Team	
Students	
Student organizations (clubs, teams, etc.)	
Parents	
Parent-teacher association	
School psychologists	
Social workers	
Community agency members	
Faith-based organizations	
Youth and community associations	
Colleges and universities	
Resources (grants, technology, etc.)	
Other	

STEP FIVE—**R**ESULTS: Restate your baseline data. Then state where your data are now. Did you meet your goal?

Restate baseline data: _____   Results (data now): _____
Met goal?: Yes_____   No _____

Questions to consider as you examine results and revise your MEASURE

Which strategies had a positive impact on the data? _____
_____
_____
_____

Which strategies should be replaced, changed, or added? _____
_____
_____
_____

Based on what you have learned, how will you revise Step Four—Stakeholders-Unite?_____
_____
_____
_____

How did your MEASURE contribute to systemic change(s) in your school and/or in your community?
_____
_____
_____
_____

STEP SIX—**E**DUCATE: Educate others as to your efforts to move data. Develop a report card that shows how the work of the school counselor(s) is connected to the mission of the schools and to student success. Following is a template for a brief report card that can be used to summarize your effort. Keep your completed report to no more than two pages for maximum impact.

(School Name) *MEASURE OF SUCCESS*

Principal: _____

School Counselor(s): _____

Enrollment: _____

Principal's Comment	Results (include any systemic change as well as specific details)
School Counselor's Comment	
Critical Data Element(s)	
	"Faces Behind the Data" (include reactions from people affected
School Improvement Issues Addressed	
Stakeholders Involved and What They Did	

NAVIANCE
a Hobsons company

Naviance is the leading provider of student success solutions for K-12 schools. Naviance is built on the belief that every student has the potential for academic and post-secondary success, and the Naviance Success Model was designed with this end in mind. The Model is based on four key values:

- **Success starts with a plan.** Every student deserves an individualized "success" plan that connects his or her learning to meaningful personal goals.

- **Success depends on raising expectations.** Students should be inspired to increase their course rigor and their expectations of themselves to better prepare for college and work.

- **Success requires meaningful data.** Schools need the right tools to monitor access to rigorous courses and track long-term outcomes like college placement and the need for remediation.

- **Success goes beyond instruction.** Students need to learn about themselves, develop a vision of their future and collaborate with adults who can provide a support system for overcoming challenges.

The Naviance Success Model is the guiding principle behind Naviance Succeed, a suite of products and services for K-12 schools and districts that promotes college and workplace readiness through increased collaboration, rigor, and transparency. Naviance Succeed integrates market-leading course, college and career planning systems that provide students with a framework to direct their own education, establish long and short-term goals and plan for post-secondary success.

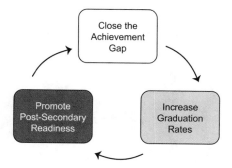

Naviance is proud to work with thousands of member schools and districts to deliver success plans for every student. To learn more, please visit www.naviance.com.

Naviance is the K-12 division of Hobsons, a subsidiary of DMG Information, which in turn is part of the Daily Mail and General Trust plc. In conjunction with Hobsons higher education services, Naviance is uniquely positioned to provide end-to-end solutions that span K-12, career education, undergraduate studies, and graduate programs.

SUBSCRIPTIONS AT A GLANCE
Save Time. Save Money. Make Better Decisions

The ERS Advantage Annual Research Service enables you to. . .

- Enhance your effectiveness as decision makers
- Make research-based, data-driven decisions with confidence
- Learn about programs and practices that will improve student achievement

Simply choose the subscription option that best meets your needs:

✓ **ERS District Advantage**—an annual research and information service that provides education leaders with timely research on priority issues in preK-12 education. We do the work so that you don't have to! For one annual fee, you will receive ERS publications and periodicals, ERS Custom Searches, and 50% discounts on ERS resources. Also, we will send your entire staff the ERS e-Bulletin and Informed Educator Series to keep them up-to-date on current educational topics and important issues. Another benefit is 24/7 FREE access to the ERS e-Knowledge Portal that contains more than 1,600 educational research-based documents, as well as additional content uploaded throughout the year.

✓ **ERS Leaders Advantage**—an individual annual service designed primarily for school administrators, and school board members who want to receive a personal copy of new ERS studies, reports, and/or periodicals published, as well as 25% discounts on other resources purchased.

✓ **Other Education Agency Subscription**—available for state associations, libraries, departments of education, service centers, and other organizations needing access to quality research and information resources and services.

We Want to be Your Research Partner. Let ERS work for you!

Your ERS Subscription benefits begin as soon as your order is received and continue for 12 months. For more detailed subscription information and pricing, contact ERS toll free at 800-791-9308, by email at ers@ers.org, or visit us online at www.ers.org!